T0315473

One More Day

One More Day

Find **Strength and Resilience** through Your Darkest Times with **Life-Saving** Tools from **Positive Psychology**

Niyc Pidgeon

HAY HOUSE

Carlsbad, California • New York City
London • Sydney • New Delhi

Published in the United Kingdom by:
Hay House UK Ltd, The Sixth Floor, Watson House,
54 Baker Street, London W1U 7BU
Tel: +44 (0)20 3927 7290; www.hayhouse.co.uk

Published in the United States of America by:
Hay House LLC, PO Box 5100, Carlsbad, CA 92018-5100
Tel: (1) 760 431 7695 or (800) 654 5126; www.hayhouse.com

Published in Australia by:
Hay House Australia Publishing Pty Ltd, 18/36 Ralph St,
Alexandria NSW 2015
Tel: (61) 2 9669 4299; www.hayhouse.com.au

Published in India by:
Hay House Publishers (India) Pvt Ltd, Muskaan Complex,
Plot No.3, B-2, Vasant Kunj, New Delhi 110 070
Tel: (91) 11 4176 1620; www.hayhouse.co.in

A catalogue record for this book is available from the British Library.

Tradepaper ISBN: 978-1-4019-7747-4
E-book ISBN: 9-781-83782-202-7
Audiobook ISBN: 9-781-83782-201-0

10 9 8 7 6 5 4 3 2 1

Printed in the United States of America

This product uses responsibly sourced papers and/or recycled materials. For more information, see www.hayhouse.com.

In loving memory of Sophie Gradon,
Chris Redhead, and Sara Hepburn.

For my niece Olivia, nephew Alfie, and for all the kids
who get to grow up in a better future world because
of the healing work we do on ourselves today.

Know that your mental health
matters, and you matter, too.

To the survivors. You made it.
Thank you for giving us hope.

To you, the reader, for holding on, harnessing hope,
choosing devotion, and finding connection.

And for keeping on going, for one more day.

Author's Note

Your mental health journey should be supported by a qualified professional. Severe mental health conditions may require a more immediate in-person intervention.

If you or a loved one are experiencing crisis right now, head to the Befrienders Worldwide website to find the contact details of your nearest support center (https://befrienders.org/find-support-now/).

Help is available. There is always someone who can listen. Speak with someone today.

Contents

Hope

Devotion

Connection

Keep Fighting

List of Exercises and Interventions

The Pact

In August 2014, I was in my car in my hometown of Newcastle, England, holding hands with my friend Sophie. We'd just left the funeral of our friend Chris, who had died by suicide. Sophie turned to me and said, 'We have to make a promise today – we can't let this happen again. This can't happen to another one of our friends.'

Looking into each other's eyes, with tears streaming down our faces, we made the pact.

A few years later, our friend Sara died by suicide.

A year after that, a coroner's report determined Sophie had died by suicide, too.

Three friends. All of them gone – lost to suicide – while I was giving motivational talks about how to live your best life. I was shattered. Because of how much Soph believed in the power of Positive Psychology and was such a supporter of my work – and, maybe most of all, because of that wrenching pact we made after Chris's funeral – her death was the hardest to process. We'd met as teenagers in Newcastle, bonding over school and nights out. Since then, we'd followed dreams that took us around the world, but we always cherished the friendships that helped form us, and we spent time together in person as much as we could.

Seeds

One of the most vivid memories of my last years in Newcastle was a lunch with my friend Chris at Jesmond Dene, a lovely park along a small river called the Ouseburn. I'd picked up takeout from my favorite deli – brown rice and salad – and we sat on a bench together, enjoying it. Chris told me how the doctors had labeled him as having bipolar disorder. He'd refused the diagnosis because he didn't want to take the medication. But he said he was feeling healthy and getting better. Our friend group had been so worried for so long. That made this conversation especially relieving. Everything was going to be OK.

Maybe more than OK! At the time, I was giving talks in Newcastle about *how to live your best possible life*. One night, a week after my joyful lunch with Chris, I'd just finished one of these talks at the Naked Deli coffee shop – the same deli where I'd picked up the healthy takeout a week before. My talk had gone so well, and I exited the shop absolutely high on life. I was really feeling this topic. *This is how you live your best possible life!* I knew exactly what I was supposed to be doing. I'd been nervous, but I'd pulled it off.

Inside my car, I pulled my phone out of my purse to give it a quick check before I drove home. I saw a TON of missed calls from my friend Caroline. I knew at once that something was terribly wrong.

I called Caroline back. She told me Chris had ended his life.

Just a week after our lovely lunch, Chris was gone.

How was I supposed to make sense of that news? Seconds after the soaring high – the uplifting energy of the crowd of people ready to start living life to the full – I was alone in my car with the news that Chris's life was over. I'd never see him again. Such a high to such a low. Whiplash.

Chris. Redhead. That was our nickname for him for as long as I could remember. How could he be gone? I'd known him since I was about 17, back when my friend Alex and I would eat a whole ham, pineapple, mushroom pizza in her car. We'd driven home from a night out, and these two guys were standing in the road. One of them was Chris. That's how we became friends.

Chris was always so upbeat. He made people around him happy. Chris had always been one of my biggest supporters. When I was preparing for a half marathon, he told me, 'I know you're gonna do your best time, Niyc. I totally believe in you and know you're gonna do it.' When I was training for that event, I'd often think, 'I'm running this for Redhead.' I still have the photo of my watch with my time as I finished the race and texted him to celebrate.

He's what kept me going, step after step. He still does to this day.

He seemed to be doing so well during our picnic lunch. *Just a week before.*

Again and again, it's the same refrain. Some of the happiest people around are the ones who are struggling the most.

In June 2019, I had just landed in Cape Town after attending a wedding in Europe when I found out about Sophie. I was about to unpack my case when my phone rang, and my world was shattered again. I turned around, went straight back to the airport, and got on a flight to the UK to be with my friends. I spent the next few weeks trying to make sense of why Sophie was the third of my friends to have died by suicide.

I remember being in tears, sat wrapped in a blanket on the sofa. *What I teach doesn't work*, I thought. *Positive Psychology doesn't work.* Sophie had always been a fierce supporter of Positive Psychology and often came to the talks I held in our local library and coffee shop. She'd taken my online courses as well. Sophie was a model. Gorgeous. She'd been crowned Miss Great Britain and had starred in a reality TV series called *Love Island*. She was always ready to cheer someone up. I knew she'd been struggling. She'd spoken openly about being bullied online and about her loneliness, not knowing if the people around her were genuine or just interested in her celebrity status. Still, she'd had access to many evidence-based Positive Psychology tools to help lift her up. Why hadn't they worked for her?

My work involved traveling the world, championing these tools to help others discover how to live well and feel better more of the time. I'd even written a book on the subject![1] Meanwhile, three of my friends – Chris, Sara, Sophie – were no longer *living*. I may have been able to run a half marathon, but I couldn't run from the enormous contradiction I felt lay at the center of my work and life.

It turns out I didn't have to.

A change in perspective

My change in perspective began when I was sitting alone, crying on my sofa, but the lesson became embodied while I was teaching the 'Meaning' pillar in my Positive Psychology Coach Academy Certification course. We were discussing positive legacy and doing a practice exercise. I was managing OK while the students were in the room with me, but as soon as I sent them into breakout rooms, I burst into tears. I'd heard from Caroline again that yet *another* friend wasn't doing well.

Another one?

'I feel like it's happening again,' I told my coaching team. In my head, I knew the importance of the work I was doing, but my heart was shattered. It felt so heavy and hard not to be able to help my best friends. What did that mean for the work I was dedicating my life to?

My colleague Ali listened to everything I said. She didn't rush to make me feel better or 'fix' the situation. Instead, she shared two simple analogies from her yoga practice. Both are metaphors for doing good work but being unable to control the outcome. The first is that when we plant and water a seed, we can't know when or how that particular plant or flower will grow. It *will* grow; it will blossom and bloom. The work we put in now will grow plants in the future. But that part isn't up to us.

The second metaphor helps us to visualize the same idea. When you shoot an arrow using a bow, you can aim in a certain direction, but you still don't know exactly where it'll land. (At least, I don't – maybe you're a better mark than me!) But if we shoot positive arrows, they'll land somewhere and help somebody.

In other words, when it comes to the good work we do, we don't always get to decide what the impact will be. I know the practices of Positive Psychology have the power and potential to shift our thinking and feeling. And alongside these teachings, I now also bring the lessons Ali brought me from her yoga class.

Both of those examples really landed for me. Planting seeds. Shooting arrows. They helped me make peace with my role and my purpose. I felt the compassion of everyone on the team as well. They were present with me, planting seeds and shooting arrows. We'll all have many opportunities to speak with people who are struggling. We can't dismiss the hope that we *might* be able to help – even if we were unable to in the past. *I'm doing something good*, I reminded myself. The energy is still out there. I just have to hold on to the bigger picture, vision, and mission.

I don't get to study positive interventions to help prevent suicide and say, 'This is going to keep my best friend from taking her life.' In fact, I'm out of the loop of being overly responsible for other people. This is a different path. What I hope to do with this book is to begin to map out a new way for society to *be*. Together, we can weave a tapestry ushering us toward a world where suicide no longer happens. We're moving, step by step, with the memory of Redhead and other loved ones who used to cheer us on, toward a day when people will say, 'Remember when people used to die by suicide?' the same way we say, 'Remember when people used to smoke on airplanes?' It'll be inconceivable that over 700,000 people a year took their own lives. A puzzling, distant memory – unbelievable that it was ever the world we lived in. *That's* my hope.

If we treat suicide as a health behavior, just like smoking, this means we can prevent it. When we recognize suicide as a *behavior*, and we remember behaviors can be changed, we realize the prevalence of suicide can be changed, too. Not everybody is aware of this approach to understanding suicide, even though it's been researched for more than 20 years.[2] Most suicidology books don't touch on it and instead focus on mental illness as the cause of suicide. The fact is that suicide is a complex problem and one that isn't going to be solved overnight. We know keeping people alive is a worthy goal, but unless we take the time to build lives worth living, our efforts at solving the problem will ultimately fail.[3] Positive Psychology helps build lives worth living.

It's easy to get stuck in the darkness and fixate on everything that's wrong. Our negativity bias brings us to that place quite efficiently. Negativity bias is the tendency in our brains to pick up on negative things more easily and dwell on them. It means we're prone to feeling criticism more strongly, recalling negative events more readily than positive ones, and dwelling on negative thoughts more often. Essentially, we pay more attention to the bad stuff, and over-inflate it, making it seem more important than it is.

Negative thinking will take you down faster than anything else. It's easier to hop into a downward spiral than an upward spiral. As we'll discuss in more detail later, you need three to five positives to counteract every one negative experience. Positive Psychology guides us toward everything that's right, and to the simple shifts we can make to feel better. Toward the light. Toward one more day and one more day and one more day after that.

We can always ask ourselves the question: *What can I do to feel a tiny bit better today?*

We live in a time when so many advances are being made in the world of suicide prevention, but these advances aren't becoming common knowledge yet. My hope is to raise awareness of the research, methods, and tools from the field of Positive Psychology that are proven to work for suicide prevention, so that this knowledge becomes part of the mainstream and accessible to everyone.

Feeling something new

Recently, I celebrated a Fourth of July holiday in Newport Beach, California, at my friend Jamie's beach house. As we walked into a restaurant, one of the songs from Chris's funeral started playing. It was Otis Redding's classic hit '(Sittin on) The Dock of the Bay.' This kind of thing happens to me a lot – I'll randomly hear songs from the services of the friends I've lost. Sometimes, I'll be out somewhere and that type of music isn't even playing and suddenly, a song with such strong emotional resonance for me will come over the speakers.

That day in Newport, I again burst into tears thinking about Chris, Sara, and Sophie. But this time felt different. This time, it wasn't the utter grief and emptiness I'd felt when I heard the news that each one had ended their lives. And it wasn't the same kind of pain I'd felt in the months and years that followed as I did my best to process losing them and figure out how to reconcile the promise of my work with the despair over losing these friends.

I was crying just as hard as those other times, but this time I was feeling something new.

'Are you all right?' my friend Orit asked.

'I'm so good,' I told her, smiling through my tears.

And I was. Because I now understood that I could be totally shattered and also inspired. I could be devastated at what I've lost but still able to find the gold within.

The emotion that comes through from loss is actually love. There's so much joy in my grief and in recalling the memories and happy times. There's so much love in loss. That's what grief is – it's love for that person, isn't it?

I'm committing to taking the steps I can take to save as many lives as possible. I'm keeping the pact I made with Sophie after Chris's funeral. The pact is this book. I'm writing it. I'm living it. And I'm keeping the promise to do what I can to honor Sophie's memory by fulfilling our shared promise.

I know that writing this book and spreading this message is my purpose and I know my friends are cheering me on. The book is an opening. It's not a solution. It's a *start*. These words are the seeds I can plant. These sentences are the arrows I can shoot. My purpose came through conflict, questioning, uncertainty, hopelessness, and a sense of powerlessness. It came from an evening in a Newcastle deli parking lot when I received the news of Redhead's death, and my joy came crashing around me. It came from me at my home in LA, devastated to hear that Sara had taken her own life as well. It came from the pain of losing Sophie after we'd made a vow never to let this happen again.

These losses birthed the biggest possible purpose and mission in my life. I don't believe the reason they died was to *serve* this mission, but I do know that this energy of hopelessness and ruin can shift into something good. From powerless to powerful. From hopeless to hopeful. From shattered to strong, committed, and devoted to this single goal. My soul's purpose came from a place of grief and a sense of failure.

You may not agree with everything I feel. What I can do is offer one perspective: what's shown to work in the science, what's worked for me. One path we can choose out of the darkness.

A path lined with seeds.

A vision of all that will one day grow.

Welcome

As a Positive Psychologist, I'm immersed in the research on how individuals, communities, and businesses thrive. Positive Psychology – the science of happiness – was developed in 2000 by the then-chair of the American Psychological Association, Martin Seligman. He identified the need for a more positive body of psychology work that focuses on human strengths and virtues instead of disorders and diseases, which was the more common focus of psychology until then. Positive Psychology explores the things that help us create good lives and tests and provides evidence for interventions, exercises, and tools that increase our well-being.

I never thought I'd become a Positive Psychologist with such a deep commitment to suicide prevention. However, after losing Chris, Sara, and Sophie, and having my own experience with suicidal ideation and a suicide attempt, I came to acknowledge and accept the call I was receiving. I wanted to use my experiences to make a positive difference in this area. I felt compelled to write this book to get the message out to more people about what it takes to survive and begin to thrive – and *how simple it is to make a start.*

If you're here, I imagine you're having a hard time right now. You're watching a loved one struggling, or you want to know how to support yourself so you can navigate any future highs and lows.

Welcome.

You've come to the right place. Pain and even torment may have spurred you to buy this book, but I hope you'll find joy in these pages.

There's a common misconception that Positive Psychology is just about being happy all the time. But the science also recognizes the value of challenge and adversity and examines how we can learn and grow through tough times. We know we can feel joy and smile in times of grief, and that even within happy moments there can be sorrow. Positive Psychology wasn't designed to either cure or prevent suicide. Yet as the science of happiness has evolved, we've been able to make a link between it and suicidology (the study of suicide, as well as suicidal and life-threatening behavior).

I offer this book as an invitation.

An exploration.

An opening.

An opportunity.

I hope you find in it the energy of adventure. That's what I'm feeling, as I write it. True, our topic is a heavy one. The stakes are life or death, literally. Around the world, over 700,000 people take their own lives each year. Suicide is the fourth leading cause of death among young people – aged 15 to 29.[1] And these figures don't include suicide attempts, which happen at a rate approximately 20 times higher.

However, our approach to addressing this topic can be filled with light. As Alan Cohen said, 'You will find truth more quickly through delight than gravity. Let out a little more string on your kite.' I love that image of the kite – tethered to the Earth, but free to soar.

A book about hope

Positive Psychology *can* save lives. It already does. And practicing it gives us the power to touch people far beyond our own close relationships and friendship groups. In the pages ahead I'll show you how, by sharing personal stories and proven tools from the science of happiness.

As I mentioned above, Positive Psychology was created to counterbalance traditional psychology, focusing on human strengths and virtues rather than disorders and diseases. It moves the focus away from what we do wrong, and what goes wrong, to what is possible instead.

What if we applied the Positive Psychology model to the topic of suicide, and instead of just looking at risk factors and causes, we started to support the process with more *protective* factors, interventions, and a focus on what *is* going right? After all, if we can prevent suicide attempts in the first place, we reduce the risk of suicide. That's why *One More Day* isn't just a book about suicide prevention but a book about hope.

If you're struggling, there *is* hope. And wherever you are on your journey it's super important to remember how far you've come. This kind of reflection is particularly resonant for those who have suffered from suicidal thoughts and found a way out. So, throughout this book, I'll also shine a light on a few survivor stories so you can read about what worked for these people when they were really struggling, too. Alongside the real-life stories you'll read here, I share simple, easy-to-use tools from Positive Psychology which can help prevent suicide, both for you, the reader, and for the people in your lives who might be having a hard time. You'll find interventions and exercises throughout, proven to boost positivity, enhance well-being, and protect mental health.

Who is this book for?

This book is for:

People who are suffering

Living through adversity and struggle can be overwhelming, and for those who also suffer with mental health conditions, it can feel 10 times worse. *One More Day* can help bring comfort and hope to people who are suffering and help them feel a bit of relief from their pain and see the potential up ahead.

Gatekeepers

One More Day can help parents, friends, teachers, therapists, coaches, and anyone who has the potential to come into contact with an at-risk person, to be better equipped to support them. Research shows that one suicide impacts 135 people,[2] and in a lifetime 20–26 percent of people will be affected by a suicide within their circle. If we can equip this group of people to know how to help someone who's struggling, we can make a major impact in this space. The personal development of gatekeepers affects their ability to see beyond the present struggle, as well as their belief in the capacity of their friend, patient, or child to change.[3] The more gatekeepers engage in Positive Psychology-based interventions themselves, the better resourced they'll be to support others and the more effective their support will be.

How to use this book

My invitation is to keep an open mind when making your way through this book. Be willing to explore different exercises and interventions and see how they feel for you. I know how it feels when you're struggling so you won't find big, intimidating chapters to slog through here. I didn't want this to be a snore fest, either! I think it'll be helpful to read through the entire book once, and perhaps circle or highlight the areas that resonate the most. Of course, you're also free to flip through the pages on any given day and see where you land. Whichever page you land on, it's going to give you a shift to feel a little better.

We can all make positive changes in this space, individually and together. By exploring the resources in this book and adopting simple practices from Positive Psychology, we can come to rely more on each other. We can equip ourselves to help each other, to interrupt patterns of hopelessness and find our way through to the other side.

I also understand that suicidal ideation comes and goes, presents differently in different people, and varies in intensity, duration, and character.[4] Positive Suicidology isn't a one-size-fits-all approach. I'm presenting the latest research along with lessons I've learned to make sure as many people as possible have access to proven tools so they can help themselves and the people they love find more reasons to live. However, I don't want you to take this guidance and navigate your life *my* way.

I want you to navigate your life *your* way. Doing so will mean understanding yourself, your habits and preferences, and your strengths. You'll choose your own path.

One of the ways I've successfully shifted away from suicidal thinking is by leaning into who I am and focusing on my strengths. I'm imaginative and love big-picture thinking. I also love to take what I've learned and use it to help others change their thinking. It seems perfect for somebody who loves to learn and write. Determining strengths is a key part of *One More Day* – recognizing we're all good at something.

What *One More Day* means for you

I chose the title *One More Day* because it captures the energy of hope I want to emerge through every section of the book. But *One More Day* isn't just the title of this book; it's an entire process in itself – a framework, rooted in Positive Psychology, that I hope will change the course of suicide prevention as we know it, permanently. So when I use the term One More Day going forward, know that it applies to both this book *and* the process as a whole.

One More Day offers comfort, and helps you see the potential up ahead. Holding on to hope, devoting ourselves to self-care by practicing research-based Positive Psychology tools for lifting our moods, and coming back to connect with the present, and with each other, will help us to live more fully and keep going one more day.

The One More Day framework is broken down into three core concepts: hope, devotion, and connection. Imagine three concentric circles. At the center lies 'hope,' which is the thread that will carry us through this process. Surrounding 'hope' is a circle representing 'devotion.' Finally, surrounding both 'hope' and 'devotion' is an outer circle symbolizing 'connection.'

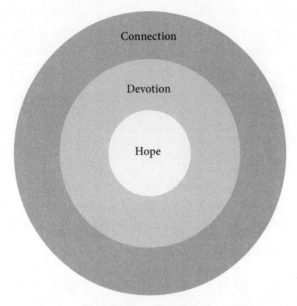

One More Day Framework

Hope is a feeling of trust, desire, and belief in success and fulfillment. Hope has to come first in this framework because without hope, you either don't start or you want to give up. Imagine hope as the tiny seed that grows. Devotion is your devotion to yourself, to making it through one more day, to your positive mental health journey. Connection is your connection with yourself, a higher power, with your purpose, and with others around you. Talking helps. Finding places you feel you belong helps. Each time you practice this simple One More Day framework, you'll strengthen yourself and amplify your hope. Need something to believe in? Believe in hope.

Hope, Devotion, Connection Exercise

Journaling can enhance your mental and physical well-being and health, so it's a great habit to start if you haven't already. Here are some prompts to get you started. Pick whichever ones speak to you and write down some thoughts – either by hand or using the 'notes' section of your phone. Writing with a pen and paper is proven to be more powerful because of the brain-body connection. But we're not being fussy. We just want to get going here.

Begin with just three minutes; it doesn't have to be a lengthy session. But you do need to start.

Hope

–   What positive associations do you have with the word 'hope?'

–   What are you hoping for today?

–   What do you hope to bring into your life in the next year?

–   List five places, ideas, people, memories, or objects that give you a hopeful feeling.

Devotion

–   What positive associations do you have with the word 'devotion?'

–   What are you devoted to for yourself?

–   What are you devoted to for your relationships?

–   What are you devoted to for the world?

–   Where would you like to practice putting more energy of devotion?

Connection

- What positive associations do you have with the word 'connection?'

- What makes you feel most connected with yourself?

- What makes you feel more connected to others?

- What was a recent conversation or experience where you felt a strong connection to someone else?

- What is a connection with someone else you desire to strengthen? What could you do to strengthen it?

Keep your journal or notes nearby as you read this book. It's a wonderful way for you to internalize the lessons and make them your own.

If you read my first book, *Now Is Your Chance,* you may remember the Brain Dump exercise, a kind of mind-declutter. This practice is super simple: Take out your journal or open the 'notes' section on your phone, set a timer for five minutes, and write down anything and everything that's spinning around in your head – from a grocery list to an idea for a story you want to write. Just dump it all out on the page. It doesn't get much easier, and it's a great way to clear your mind. Plus, it's something you can come back to again and again.

As we move through *One More Day,* we're tackling a topic that's more complex and nuanced than creating a life filled with joy. We hope to arrive at that place eventually – and help others do the same – but the context here is the awareness that many people are struggling to stay alive, let alone live that life joyfully. This book doesn't run from complexities and questions. In fact, it invites and welcomes them. I'll be honest when I struggle with uncertainty and pitfalls along the way. (Sometimes I feel like I'm getting the shit kicked out of me daily, so trust me, there are plenty of pitfalls I've overcome for me to share.)

As we work together to grow your physical, emotional, and spiritual resources, I hope you'll start feeling some of the benefits of working with the tools in *One More Day*. These include:

- feeling more connected to others

- living more mindfully

- embracing joy

- committing to a centering spiritual practice

- discovering how to shift your mood

- gathering tools to support yourself and others

- being inspired by personal stories

- harnessing your strengths in the service of suicide prevention

- finding space to breathe

- increasing attention to positivity and being intentional about finding it in your day

- developing healthy routines

- finding purpose and meaning in your life

- joining (and starting) more conversations

- increasing your long-term resilience and well-being

- being part of a powerful movement celebrating life

- harnessing the feeling and power of hope

In the upcoming sections, as you work through the practices and take notes on the reflections, keep thinking about what you hope to learn, what practices you want to devote yourself to, and what connections you can make. By making simple shifts each day, you can create a more positive trajectory for your life.

The subject of suicide seems to throw up more questions than answers. I'm hoping that this book will help you feel like you have more choices, more opportunities, and more hope, even on the days you don't have all the answers.

What this book is not

This is important: *One More Day* is a tool to support your mental health journey and suicide prevention. It *is not* a crisis intervention tool. In a crisis, follow the suicide protocol and call your local crisis hotline. (*See pages 229–231 for suicide hotline information.*) Call your country's emergency services in life-threatening situations.

One More Day isn't a definitive guide to suicide prevention research. There are some amazing books I've read and learned so much from, and I've listed some of them for you in the Recommended Reading section at the end of the book. (*See page 227*).

Hope

The Ripple

'Each time a man stands up for an ideal, or acts to improve the lot of others, or strikes out against injustice, he sends forth a tiny ripple of hope, and crossing each other from a million different centers of energy and daring, those ripples build a current that can sweep down the mightiest wall of oppression and resistance.'

Robert F. Kennedy

Research has shown that Positive Psychology doesn't just impact the person who applies an intervention for themselves; there's a ripple effect that extends wider and further, where the benefits to well-being are also experienced by family, friends, colleagues, and anyone who comes in contact with the person changing their life. The closer you are to someone who practices Positive Psychology, the more likely you are to experience positive improvements in well-being.[1]

Isn't that amazing – the ripple effect of this science? Pause for a minute and take that in. It makes me smile, just knowing the impact these changes can make in our lives and the lives of those around us.

Research shows that positive emotions are contagious as well. When someone works with Positive Psychology tools and increases their well-being, we see that the quality of their interactions with others increases too. A study from Yale University showed that positive emotional contagion had a significant influence on individual attitudes and group dynamics – we're continuously influencing each other's moods, which also then influences judgments and behaviors.[2]

Even tiny positive actions can ripple out. Ingrid Fetell Lee gives a lovely example in her uplifting book *Joyful: The Surprising Power of Ordinary Things to Create Extraordinary Happiness*: 'A whimsical outfit might prompt a smile,' Lee writes, 'which inspires a chance kindness toward a stranger, which helps someone who is struggling to get through her day.'[3]

Remember the seeds analogy from the opening of this book? Planting them is an act filled with so much hope. A whimsical outfit could be a seed. So could offering to water your neighbors' plants while they're out of town. Showing kindness to one person fills them up a little so that they can show kindness to someone else.

I'm reminded of the poignant speech Robert F. Kennedy gave in 1966 in Cape Town, South Africa on its Day of Affirmation (a portion of which opens this chapter). The speech came to be known as his 'Ripple of Hope' speech. Each time you take an action that improves someone else's life, you're sending out a ripple. Together we, too, can harness 'a million different centers of energy and daring.' Energy and daring. I love the sound of that!

'Ripples of hope' may seem insignificant at first. But continue to trust in the energy and the power of the ripples and you'll begin to see evidence of the current and positive cascade. It's like a tapestry, as my friend Rolando would attest. Rolando is an Omo Awo – someone who is a Babalawo in training. A Babalawo is a spiritual figure, often considered a priest, within the Ifa tradition. During dinner together in the Middle East (on what became a pivotal trip for my life and so powerful for the birthing of this book) Rolando described our connections to each other and the events in our lives – good and bad – as unique, essential, purposeful, and interconnected threads that together make up the beautiful picture our lives are meant to be. I loved that. For me, it perfectly encapsulates the ethos of *One More Day*.

I believe that with this movement we can begin weaving a new way of life. We can choose to energize expansion rather than energize suffering. One positive shift can lead to another and another.

What Kennedy's metaphor and the word tapestry remind me is that transformation isn't linear. When creating a tapestry, we sometimes miss stitches along the way. We may lose our path from time to time in life, too. Any given day may not turn out the way we want, but there's strength in continuing stitch after stitch, in pursuing our vision collectively. As we all become more psychologically, spiritually, and emotionally resourced, we grow in our power to lift ourselves and each other up for one more day.

An Invitation

In the following chapters, I'm going to introduce interventions and exercises from Positive Psychology that can help us create positive change on a global scale. When you're struggling, these activities will show you how to find a little more light in your day. In addition, incorporating them will allow you to create a healthy routine that will help you keep going, enrich your life and, ultimately, lead to greater flourishing. That greater flourishing will in turn enhance your ability to impact others in positive ways. The idea is that you'll empower yourself with these practices and then go on to support others and, in some cases, perhaps teach others how to practice them as well.

Centering yourself with daily tools means you'll be better able to serve as an anchor for someone else who's losing their way. Maybe instead of offering advice when in the presence of someone in deep pain, you'll have the resources, because of the work you've done on yourself – the walk you took that morning, the deep breaths before you got to work – to be a sounding board, offering love and compassion. Positive Psychology can give you the ability to be present and allow a friend to speak without feeling judged.

Survivor Story

What helped you get through one more day?

I'm managing because of skills I've been lucky enough to learn, such as mindfulness and meditation. Exercise really helps, and talking to other women helps.

Survivor

Of course, we're all at different points on our mental health journey. Emotions ebb and flow, thoughts come and go, and some days are going to be better than others. Resource yourself first before you think about helping others – you're the most important thing.

Survivor Story

What helped you get through one more day?

I talked to my husband, wrote in a journal for a little bit, and wrote letters to people about how I felt and how they made me feel (but I never sent them). I started to believe in ME, and that I'm good enough and loved by my husband.

Survivor

Not everyone feels OK having a conversation about something as difficult as suicide. We should always be mindful that a person may have trauma related to the topic that they haven't yet processed. For that reason, we have to be responsible about how we approach the subject. I like to ask permission. Sometimes people ask me what I'm working on, and before I jump straight into the topic, I ask, 'Is it all right if I share with you some of the context around the stories and intentions for the book?' I let them know there's an intersection between the findings of Positive Psychology and suicide prevention that I want to bring forward to help more people.

Perhaps it'll be all right to have this discussion, or perhaps it would be better to wait for another time.

It's easy enough to ask.

Be curious.

Be patient.

Be gentle.

With yourself and others. I recognize that just because I'm taking a stand for suicide prevention and it's normal for me to get deep into conversation about this topic, it doesn't mean it's normal for everyone. We get to walk the path together gently.

Welcome someone into this conversation, if they're open to it.

Tiny Tools

I was at dinner recently at a friend's house when the topic of suicide came up. My friend shared with me that during a particularly low period she'd considered taking her own life as well. I was surprised to hear that because she's so powerful, such a go-getter, so energized, happy, and light. I wasn't even aware that she'd been suffering.

It's often those who appear the most energetic and light that are suffering the most. And yet, there's still something jarring about confronting this duality – a person who appears so cheerful and ready to take on the world, but meanwhile has contemplated leaving it. I suppose it's one of the unending puzzles of suicide. It's also one I've learned to release – in part, to align with a focus on what we can actively do to create a positive change. Instead of focusing on why suicidal thinking strikes some people and not others, let's direct our energy toward the positive steps we can take.

I paused to give my friend space as she shared. I then asked what it was that made her keep going.

She told me she'd been looking for her phone to text her husband and kids goodbye. She didn't have a pen and paper and she became so focused on finding her phone that it stopped her in her tracks. It stopped her for long enough that the thought of taking her own life stopped, too. Suicide can be a 'fleeting thought' – keep going and the thought will go away. I look back on the times I've thought about taking my own life and I see how temporary the thought was. When you know the thought will go away, it'll help you keep going for one more day. Don't make a permanent decision based on temporary feelings. Suicidal thinking won't last for ever. It will pass and you'll be able to keep going. It's going to pass when you know that you can keep going one more day.

The search for a cell phone.

Such a *tiny* thing – yet it provided a sense of purpose for long enough to usher her through a terrible moment. It opened the space for a new thought to enter her head. It interrupted the sense of total desperation she'd felt just moments earlier and set her on a new path.

Now I'm not recommending you hide your phone from yourself when you're at your lowest point (or hide someone else's). Your phone is likely your lifeline. Remember if you're feeling suicidal, or know someone who is, flip to pages 229–231 for the crisis hotlines. Deepak Chopra, Gabriella Wright, and Poonacha Machaiah's 'Never Alone' initiative also has a text chat function to support people in crisis – and has already helped save thousands of lives through its AI interface.

Let's think about the impact one tiny thing can have. Like the seeds I wrote about earlier, a tiny thing can be immensely powerful. It can mean the difference between life and death. Could a walk outside shift your mood? A few minutes of slow, deep breathing? Listening to a favorite song?

Survivor Story

What helped you get through one more day?

Music – words in songs mean a lot to me, knowing others have been through pain and have moved through it.

The second time, specifically, it was my husband who got me through. He came into the room just in time and he helped me talk things through. He allowed my brain to clear and get a plan together instead.

Survivor

In Positive Psychology we talk about positivity boosters, simple things that can help you catch your vibe in your day. I like to think of them as Tiny Tools. Their tiny-ness makes them feel doable. They're tools that are always available for you to grab. This is the essence of Positive Psychology. It's not about winning the lottery by doing one intervention one time and expecting to have it all sorted. It's really about building a magical castle one brick at a time, and understanding that the steps are simple, they work, *and*, you have to start.

Tiny Tools list

OK, now I'd like to share my Tiny Tools list. You can take any of my ideas or create your own. Or both. It feels so good to work your way through a simple task and then check it off. *OK, cool,* you'll think. *I've done something good today.* Can we use these Tiny Tools to catch people before they get into a big decline? Can we get them to shift enough so that they're able to see another point of view?

Here is a checklist of small positive actions you can take:

- Go for a walk.

- Find an accountability partner.

- Check in with yourself.

- Ask about good things.

- Turn your phone off, or put it on Do Not Disturb, between 8 p.m. and 8 a.m.

- Drink more water.

- Meditate or listen to a guided visualization.

- Make your bed.

- Enjoy a hot drink.

- Do a breath work exercise.

- Send a gratitude text.

- Create a Good Person Inventory (GPI).

- Use a dry brush.

- Draw yourself a bath and use Epsom salts.

- Shake your entire body.

- Dance!

- Get outdoors and into natural sunlight.

- Practice Qi Gong.

- Read 10 pages of a book.

- Have an orgasm.

- Repeat a prosperity chant.

- Journal for three minutes.

- Take a vitamin supplement.

- Do a 10-minute workout.

- Have a cold plunge, an ice bath, a cold shower, or splash your face with cold water.

- Water the plants.

- Perform self-massage.

- Listen to my three-minute 'Harnessing Hope' breath practice, which you can find in the audiobook version of this book or on my website, along with other helpful resources: www.niyc.com/tinytools.

The list isn't supposed to be exhaustive – or exhausting! You don't have to do them all. Just choose a few that feel easy and fun and try them! You can add other things that give you a positivity boost. The simple act of checking something off a list will give you a psychological sense of accomplishment. Plus, you know these things are good for you, so you're creating micro shifts toward better days.

Some of these tools are obvious and some may be less familiar to you. Do what you can. On tough days, it can be challenging to remember to take a step and choose what's good for you – now you have your Tiny Tools list to help. Let's look at some of these tools in a little more detail.

Go for a Walk

Yes. That's it! Get your steps in. Take steps around your neighborhood. Walk outside your office during a lunch break. Walk to the post office instead of driving. When I track my steps and I'm mindful of the boost it gives to my vitality, it provides me with a positive focus for the day. Some people like to see the health data on their phones. Others enjoy mindfully soaking up the season or listening to a podcast. You do what works for you.

The point is to put one foot in front of the other. Some steps are better than no steps, today.

I used to think of walking as taking time away from my work, but now I see it as time to boost my creativity, catch up on voice notes, or even take a call for one of the investments or businesses for which I consult. Letting go of my stories and the rigidity in my daily routines helped me find more joy, more peace, and it also means I actually get more done by stacking tasks and Tiny Tools together!

It's well known that physical activity can boost your mood.[1] Getting into nature and moving your body is a powerful intervention that activates a lot of positivity boosters. You have access to a sense of awe from the natural environment and green spaces and a sense of accomplishment from doing something good for yourself. And it doesn't have to feel like you're running a marathon or you're really out of breath – hiking brings the vibes! It's great for you whatever your level of fitness.

Survivor Story

What helped you get through one more day?

I joined a running club and a gym. I found a job I love for a company that appreciates me and encourages and accommodates my passion for fitness.

Survivor

Even just a 10-minute walk has been shown to improve mood.[2] And here's a cool fact: We have something in our bodies called the 'hope molecule.' That's the name scientists give to the hormones your muscles secrete into your bloodstream when you exercise, which makes your brain more resilient to stress. When you flex a muscle or stretch, when you walk around and move your body, you activate the hope molecule. Beautiful, isn't it?

Activating the hope molecule

I don't think I'll ever write a book that doesn't include some sort of nod to – or great big flashing light for – the importance and power of moving our bodies. With my 10 years as a personal trainer, five years of university study with a specialty in the psychology of the body (and a lifetime of self-experimentation to go with it), I know for certain that moving your body is one of the simplest and most effective ways to move your mood.

Exercise works to reduce depression, anxiety, and distress for the mentally healthy population, as well as those diagnosed with mental health disorders and chronic disease. A summary of research shows that all exercise is effective: Harder workouts give larger positive effects, lifting weights is best for reducing depression, and mind-body exercises such as yoga are most effective for reducing anxiety.[3] Moving your body boosts hope. Besides taking a walk outside, here are five simple ways you can move right now:

- Tense and then relax the muscles in each part of your body, starting at your feet and going all the way up to your head.
- Lay on the floor or your bed with your knees bent and feet flat. Drop your knees to one side then the other.
- Stand up then sit down again.
- Dance to your favorite song.
- Walk up and down the stairs.

I guarantee you'll feel a little bit better.

Survivor Story

What helped you get through one more day?

Talking with strangers helps me – and swimming in the ocean.

Survivor

Find an accountability partner

Create a common goal with a buddy. It can be something simple, like 'drinking enough water,' or something more ambitious, like completing a triathlon. This is a free, powerful mental health tool. Just by aligning and sharing your goals with someone else, the chances of accomplishing them skyrocket.

When I've been struggling, I've really benefited from a friend calling me and telling me we're going out for a walk together. Leaving the house felt like a lot at the time, but I always felt so much better afterward. It also strengthened the bond in our friendship through the quality time we spent together, and increased the gratitude I felt for that friend who cared enough to come and scoop me out of the house. Do you need to find your person – someone who will get you moving? Or perhaps you can be that person to encourage somebody else?

Once you've found your accountability partner, set up a plan for reaching the goal and figure out how you want to keep each other accountable. Will you call or text? How often? Do you want to keep track of the time you put toward reaching the goal or record certain benchmarks (e.g. swam 20 laps today)? It's as easy as sending a quick message before you turn off your phone at night: *Did you get outside today? Did you get your steps in today?* If one or both of you haven't got those steps in or got into nature for at least 10 minutes, then maybe you can do it together as you chat on the phone. You'll be making progress toward your goal and soaking up the benefits of social support at the same time. Researchers from Massachusetts General Hospital named social connection as the *most important* variable to protect against depression.[4]

Let me tell you about one of my accountability partners. I have a friend in Australia named James. When he shared with me that he was training for a half marathon, I thought, *Fuck it! I'll do one, too.* I needed a positive focus. So, we ran a half marathon 'together' on opposite sides of the world, and we checked in with each other during our training. It made it fun. I needed to go for a run most days, and James did as well. On nights where I didn't feel like it, it was my commitment to James that pushed me out the door, knowing he was going to ask me: Did you get your run in? I was always so glad I did it, not just so I could say 'yes' to James, but because after the run I felt so much better. I could think more clearly. I slept really well. So many benefits, all from that run that I did because I was accountable to someone else to do it.

Check in with yourself

So, how are you really feeling today?

1. Rate yourself from one to 10, with one being not good at all, and 10 being the best you could possibly feel.

2. Then choose how you feel from the following list of emotions. Write down as many as you think are relevant, then choose which best describes the way you're feeling right now.

Accepting	Daring	Fortunate
Adventurous	Delighted	Fragile
Affectionate	Depleted	Frazzled
Afraid	Depressed	Free
Aggravated	Despondent	Frightened
Agitated	Determined	Frustrated
Aloof	Disappointed	Fulfilled
Anguish	Discouraged	Furious
Anxious	Disdain	Gloomy
Appreciative	Disgruntled	Gracious
Apprehensive	Dissatisfied	Grateful
Ashamed	Distant	Grief
Bitter	Disturbed	Grouchy
Blessed	Eager	Grounded
Bliss	Ecstatic	Guilty
Bored	Edgy	Happy
Brave	Empathy	Heartbroken
Burned out	Empty	Helpless
Calm	Enchanted	Hesitant
Capable	Encouraged	Hopeful
Caring	Energized	Hopeless
Centered	Engaged	Hostile
Compassionate	Enthusiastic	Humbled
Concerned	Exasperated	Humiliated
Confident	Excited	Impatient
Confused	Exhausted	Impotent
Contempt	Expectant	Incapable
Content	Exploring	Indifferent
Cranky	Fascinated	Inhibited
Curious	Fear	Inspired
Cynical	Forlorn	Interested

Intrigued	Proud	Strong
Invigorated	Questioning	Suspicious
Involved	Radiant	Teary
Irate	Rattled	Tender
Irritated	Reflective	Terrified
Isolated	Refreshed	Thankful
Lethargic	Regretful	Thrilled
Listless	Rejected	Tight
Lively	Rejuvenated	Touched
Lonely	Relaxed	Trapped
Longing	Reluctant	Trusting
Loving	Remorseful	Uneasy
Lucky	Removed	Ungrounded
Melancholy	Renewed	Unhappy
Moody	Resentful	Unsure
Mortified	Resigned	Upset
Moved	Resistant	Useless
Nervous	Restless	Valiant
On edge	Safe	Vibrant
Optimistic	Satisfied	Victimized
Outraged	Scared	Vindictive
Overwhelmed	Self-conscious	Vulnerable
Panic	Self-loving	Warm
Paralyzed	Sensitive	Weak
Passionate	Serene	Weary
Patient	Shaken	Withdrawn
Peaceful	Shocked	Worn out
Perplexed	Shut down	Worried
Pissed off	Skeptical	Worthless
Playful	Sorrowful	Worthy
Powerless	Sorry	Yearning
Present	Stimulated	

3. Share with one person how you're feeling today. You could even ask them to do the same!

Ask about good things

Here's an idea for kicking off an uplifting conversation. Ask a friend three things that were good about their morning, their weekend, their last vacation, or new work project – whatever makes sense.

When I'm on the phone with someone, I love to ask, 'What was the best thing from your morning?' or 'What was the highlight of your weekend?' instead of simply 'How are you?' We all know the way 'How are you?' can lead to a scripted little back-and-forth. Instead, these questions automatically stimulate our sense of positivity and gratitude. Sometimes people are caught off guard at first, but in a good way. They don't always expect someone to *actually* want to hear about their morning. But I can tell it makes them feel good to know someone is genuinely interested in hearing about their lives.

Often when we're asked an open-ended 'How are you?' we jump to something challenging or annoying going on. This is our negativity bias at work. But when the question is framed with joy, something shifts.

What are you enjoying about your work right now? What are you most looking forward to tomorrow?

In a way, it's a version of celebrating our strengths and practicing gratitude, calling forth the bright spots in our lives rather than drawing attention to things that might simply be neutral or even bringing us down.

Drink more water

Drinking water might seem like common sense and as if you're going to do it anyway, so why add it to the list? But how often do you feel tired or realize you haven't drunk enough yet? The effects of dehydration include increased anxiety, stress, depression, and confusion.[5] Plus, reminding yourself you did drink water, and being able to check it off on your list will activate your sense of accomplishment. The small wins matter – take them and celebrate them.

Meditate or listen to a guided visualization

If you're not sure where to start, you can find some meditations and guided visualizations on my website, along with other helpful resources: www.niyc.com/tinytools. I also love listening to Abraham Hicks. Abraham is a collection of channeled voices from a non-physical plane of higher consciousness that come through Esther Hicks. You can find all kinds of soothing meditations and pep talks from them on YouTube.

Enjoy a hot drink

Starting your day with a warm drink like lemon water, tea, or bone broth feels like a cozy hug in a mug. As a reformed member of the 5 a.m. club, I've loved switching my intense 6 a.m. workouts for a slower pace. While I still love waking up early, I now savor the stillness and quiet instead of feeling like I have to *go go go* as soon as I get up. Drinking a hot drink nourishes your nervous system and can give you a feeling of calm. I love lemon water for its alkalizing and anti-inflammatory properties, and bone broth for its benefits to digestion and gut health – I can literally feel the soothing effect as I drink! Bone broth also supports sleep and immunity and is said to be anti-aging and full of collagen, which supports your skin and bones.

Do a breath work exercise

A three-minute Ego Eradicator Kundalini breath work practice is my favorite morning energizer to help connect and raise my vibes. Here's how to do it:

- Sit cross-legged and raise your arms up above your head at 60-degree angles, with your fingertips curled to touch the pads of your hands and your thumbs stretched out.

- The breath is a rapid outward and inward breath known as the breath of fire. I find it easier to focus on powerfully breathing out and drawing my navel in at the same time, and then the in-breath takes care of itself.

- Close your eyes and play a song for 3 minutes to help raise your energy. After 3 minutes take a deep inhale, touch your thumbs together above your head and stretch out your fingers above you. Exhale and sweep your arms down and out to the sides to touch the floor.

Don't practice this one if you're pregnant or on the first few days of your menstrual cycle; just choose slow, deep breathing instead.

I've filmed a video showing you how to do this practice and you can find it on my website, along with other helpful resources: www.niyc.com/tinytools.

Send a gratitude text

If you read my first book, *Now Is Your Chance*, you'll know that I LOVE dropping G-Bombs. Gratitude has been proven the world over to help you feel good and boost your well-being. That's why I practice it every day! My friend Spencer messaged me on my birthday and called me the Queen of Gratitude. If I get to be crowned as the queen of anything, I'm pretty happy with gratitude being it!

You might have heard about keeping a gratitude list for yourself, but we now also know that gratitude is stronger when it's shared. A study from The University of California in 2022 compared the effects of writing a private gratitude letter, texting a friend with gratitude, or sharing gratitude on social media. The students who texted messages of gratitude showed the biggest boosts in social connectedness and support.[6] It makes sense this would work on a particularly 'bad' day, too, where you might not feel like writing out a long letter, and sharing anything on social media just feels like a mountain to climb (I've been there!). But on those days, texting just one person with a grateful heart? That's something I believe you can do.

One thing I often choose to check off within my day is messaging someone else with gratitude. It's quick, simple, and it almost always moves me to tears. A friend of mine who's also in the Positive Psychology world once said to me, 'You know you've had a good day when you've laughed hard, felt inspired, and been moved to tears.' This Tiny Tool definitely does that for me – and it works both ways.

Why not choose one person right now and text them to share something you're grateful for about them. Perhaps it's special memories you've enjoyed together, maybe they always make you laugh, or they might be the person you've never really properly thanked, just for them being them. On the mornings I do this, I always feel better connected with my day. Texting gratitude reminds you of what's important and gives you a boost you can really feel.

Gratitude Connection Ritual

– Write down three things you're grateful for about another person.

– Share what you've written with that person via a text message.

– That's it – you've just done the Gratitude Connection Ritual!

During a Mastermind in Dubai, I asked my students to try this Gratitude Connection Ritual. We'd celebrated Diwali the evening before and were talking about Bhai Dooj, which is the second day of Diwali and celebrates the bond between siblings. I asked everyone to think of three things they were grateful for about their siblings and, as well as sharing with our group, I invited them to text their sibling and share it with them. I did it as well. What happened was so beautiful. Not only did the practice of sending the gratitude text move us all emotionally, but the replies from our siblings made us laugh and also cry. Of course, you can practice this as a ritual with anybody in your life to access the positive effect; it's not exclusive to family members.

Gratitude Rampage

A variation on this exercise that I love is the Gratitude Rampage. The Gratitude Rampage is a text or message flow between you and another person. You each share one thing you're grateful for and take it in turns, going back and forth, sharing things you are both grateful for. As the momentum and energy build, this process feels really fun!

I remember walking back to my hotel in Miami during a work trip and practicing the Gratitude Rampage with my colleague Mel. We started slowly with one thing each, then found ourselves firing a long list of gratitudes back and forth to each other. I actually wound up feeling grateful for gratitude itself and was in tears for the rest of my walk home.

One night as I was working on this book, my friend Travis sent me a voice note. He and his wife Jade had been reading *Now Is Your Chance* together and reflecting on their experience of each chapter and tool. Travis shared the most beautiful message of gratitude that took me on a roller coaster of emotions, from tears to laughter, to tears again. I was moved so powerfully by that simple voice note that I saved it so I could listen back to it again.

Create a Good Person Inventory (GPI)

I also popped Travis's voice note into my GPI (Good Person Inventory) folder on my phone so I can listen to it whenever I need a positivity boost. Sometimes when life feels tough, it's easy to be too hard on yourself. I know when I've been struggling, I've felt like I'm doing a really bad job of everything, but thinking like this is only going to make you feel worse. That's why I created the GPI photo album on my phone, where I save all the good things that will remind me I'm a good person, doing my best every day.

In this album, I've saved screenshots when friends have shared messages of gratitude and old photos from the beginning of my journey as a reminder of how far I've come. I've also added a message from *The Daily Stoic* from the day of my birthday entitled 'This is what we're here for,' which reminds me that although life is challenging and unfair, we're capable of overcoming adversity and enduring tough times because we carry the resilience and strength of our ancestors within us.

I made the rule that my GPI can't include anything work-related, but of course, you get to decide what to put in your own GPI folder. I suggest that you start this right now! Create a new photo album within your phone labeled 'GPI' and add at least one photo to it which helps you feel good. It could be a memory of something you've accomplished, a symbol of a hard time you've already made it through, or something kind you did for someone, or someone did for you.

Survivor Story

What helped you get through one more day?

Life is better now because I work on my well-being every day and I put the work in because I have to. Some people are lucky; they can put less work in and feel great. I have to put more work in, and I'm OK with that now. I save myself.

Survivor

Use a dry brush

Dry brushing your body activates the lymphatic drainage system, improves skin and circulation, and increases your energy. Experiencing this kind of physical touch can help soothe your nervous system, reduce anxiety and stress, and boost your well-being. I find this simple technique helps to bring me into the present and, along with other tools, has allowed me to shift out of functional freeze. Brush your body from your extremities toward your heart: from ankle to knee, knee to groin. From wrist to elbow, elbow to shoulder. I've created a video to show you exactly how to do this, too. See: www.niyc.com/tinytools.

Practice Qi Gong

We can't expect to feel good all of the time. But by filling our day with Tiny Tools, we can start to feel good *more* of the time. One of my favorite Tiny Tools is Qi Gong. Qi Gong is a slow-flowing meditative movement practice which works with your breath and energy centers in your body. It gives me a feeling of tranquility. I felt awkward the first time I tried it – I'm generally awkward AF and as an introvert with ADHD, I sometimes don't know what to do with my arms. Qi Gong solved that!

Read 10 pages of a book

It can be really powerful to reach for your books on a daily basis. Even just reading a short section – 10 pages – is enough to help you feel accomplished and shift your mood. What are some books you find particularly motivating and uplifting? Try to keep one on hand in a place you can always reach for it. (Maybe on your bedside table.) Whenever you need a little lift, you could flip to a random page and read it. How might the words apply to your day?

Cold plunge

Cold plunging is a life hack worth its weight in gold. Cold water immersion activates the nervous system, improves mood, lowers stress, boosts immunity, and improves mental health.[7] My first ever plunge was for six minutes, and I could barely even feel the cold. I think I'd become so desensitized to pain through experiencing such high levels of stress in my life that I needed the cold therapy more than I even realized it at the time. Now I plunge most days for six to seven minutes and it makes me feel alive! The recommended protocol is 11 minutes per week broken into multiple shorter sessions.

Of course, cold plunging isn't for everyone – make sure you seek advice from your doctor or health professional before you try this for the first time. If you don't have access to a cold plunge nearby, you can start with taking a two-minute cold shower in the morning, or even just splashing your face with cold water. Cold showers have been shown to boost mood and reduce depressive symptoms, too.[8] So why not add in a two-minute cold stint at the end of your regular shower? This one simple thing can really change the way you feel.

'Harnessing Hope' breath pattern

I keep this really simple breath work audio on my phone so I can reach for it easily. Some days it's hard to think about everything you have to do, and this is why it's really important to have your Tiny Tools close to hand so you can just start with one thing. This breath work is often my one thing, because you don't even have to get out of bed to do it. You can set it as the alarm on your phone to wake up to, and just start. You don't have to sit in any particular position or do anything difficult or complex – you just breathe when the track tells you to and that's it. You can listen to my three-minute 'Harnessing Hope' breath practice in the audiobook version of this book or on my website: www.niyc.com/tinytools.

Small shifts, big results

Remember, this isn't a to-do list. It's a These-Little-Things-Will-Make-You-Feel-Better list. I enjoy being fluid and leaning into what feels good at any given moment. No matter how many or how few Tiny Tools you do, you're guaranteed to feel a little better than you did before.

Small shifts can create big results. The things that you do daily matter the most, and your little daily habits are going to compound over time to build a better you. When you keep taking a small positive step every day, it's going to grow into something much larger. You're going to notice when you look back that it was your small, consistent, daily actions that added up to get big results. Sure, it might feel tough when you start, but it's like building muscle. You just have to start and be consistent, moving forward each day. Then you'll hit a tipping point, and you'll gain momentum. Just like a fitness transformation, you'll eventually notice your own 'before' and 'after.' Most people won't ever see the work you put in behind the scenes on your mental health journey, and they don't have to. You'll know, and that's enough.

When you remember the compound effect, you remember to keep moving – just take a step, and then another, and then another.

What's one positive step you can take for yourself toward your goals today?

Looking over the list, which items resonate with you? What might you like to try, maybe even right now? How about putting the kettle on and picking out a nice tea? Or turning on your favorite music and dancing around your house. What about picking up a book and reading 10 pages? Maybe while you ride a stationary bike! This is what I call task-stacking – getting two positive things done at the same time.

After you've had a chance to check a few Tiny Tools off your list, thank yourself. Take the moment to recognize what you've accomplished. At some point in the day, I like to look over the check marks on my list and think, *I'm doing really good. I took three positive steps already.*

One thing that helps me make headway on this list is one of the items *on* the list – keeping my phone off (or on Do Not Disturb with exceptions for emergency contacts) between 8 p.m. and 8 a.m. To be honest, I do need my team to support me with this some days and tell me to put my phone away for the night, so this isn't about being perfect. I then usually wake up when the sun comes up and I ease into my day. It's amazing how peaceful it feels to have this break from the outside world. It makes you feel like you have so much extra time! Prioritize yourself and take care of your nervous system before you get pulled into other people's priorities and distractions.

With any Tiny Tool, the hardest part is actually doing it. But once you create the habit, you'll strengthen the positive association, and feel a little bit of relief. Think about it as building positive patterns.

Reflection

- What felt good about trying these Tiny Tools?

- Which Tiny Tools connect you to yourself most?

- Which tools make you feel uplifted?

- Which tools connect you to a feeling of hopefulness?

Highlight your favorite Tiny Tools or write them down and pin them to your notice board or fridge. You could also list them in your daily planner or your digital calendar. Just make sure the list is somewhere handy. And, if possible, look at it *before* you check your emails in the morning.

Maybe some of these ideas won't do the trick. You might find yourself aligning with a prosperity chant and thinking, *Yes! Let's do this!* Or you might find that it's just not landing for you. Maybe you put on an Abraham Hicks meditation and you think, *What on earth is this going on about?* All of this is fine. All of this is *good*, in fact, because it's moving you forward. Learning what we don't like now (and that can always change) helps us zero in on what we *do* like, and how we want to feel. It's all getting us closer to where we want to be.

In Positive Psychology, we talk about the person/activity fit, a theory from Sonja Lyubomirsky's book *The How of Happiness.*[9] Some interventions will feel better than others. It's different for all of us. It's like choosing your workout – some people enjoy boxing, others prefer dancing. We're choosing our own adventure here. We're testing things, trying things, seeing what works and what doesn't. Experimenting. Finding out which tools lead to breakthroughs and which feel kind of blah. Approach these practices with a sense of playfulness. (And enjoy the endorphins that a sense of playfulness will help your body release!)

If you stay stagnant, the universe isn't going to meet you. Forward motion – no matter how tiny – allows the universe to support you. So, what can we do when we're feeling stuck?

We can choose simplicity.

We can pick up a tool and move forward. We can do something we love on a consistent basis. Over time, the effects will start to amplify each other.

If you're already feeling pretty good, these tools will help you feel even better. What's also great about this journey is knowing that the more familiar you are with these tools, the more equipped you'll be to share them with others. When someone near you is struggling, you'll be able to share what you tried and what you've learned. This is part of embodying and integrating the ideas of Positive Psychology, so you're positioned to help spread their benefits to others through your light energy and example and your enhanced ability to support someone else in their journey.

Many of these Tiny Tools will sound too simple to make a difference, but I promise they'll help. Come back to this list again and again. These tools are always here for you. You just have to be willing to reach for them.

Hard Days

I study and teach positivity for a living, and I've done my best to integrate the science of happiness into my life, but not every day is perfect. Anyone can struggle with mental health, no matter how great their life might seem. Plus, we rarely know what someone is actually facing day to day. We sometimes judge people's happiness based on the highlight reel of their lives on social media. That's one reason it's so critical for us to have more conversations with the people around us, in our reality, with our families and our friendship groups. It's why we need to listen, and why we need to ask questions.

And listen again.

When we *truly* listen, we uncover what's really going on in the lives of the people around us.

Even right now – while I'm loving writing this book, the sun is shining, and I'm feeling so good after a run – I'm feeling the weight of tremendous pressures in my life. Being on a positive mental health journey is available for everybody, no matter what life circumstances you're experiencing right now. Some days feel hard, and I can see exactly which patterns or stressors are affecting my ability to function. Other days just feel harder, and there's no real explanation for it. I keep remembering to take steps and keep moving forward.

You may be familiar with the instinctual stress responses, commonly referred to in the fields of psychology and trauma studies as fight, flight, freeze, or fawn.[1] These responses show how our bodies respond to perceived danger:

- Fight: facing the danger and responding with aggression to overpower the threat.

- Flight: removing yourself from the threat by physically moving away to try and save yourself.

- Freeze: feeling stuck and unable to fight or flight, being still until the threat passes.

- Fawn: submissive response of avoiding and becoming agreeable so you can survive. The fawn response is often seen in situations involving chronic stress or abuse, and when fight, flight, or freeze aren't possible.

The more I learned, the more aware I became that I'd been existing in a state of functional freeze. Since seeing the signs, I've been able to shift my nervous system using somatic release exercises, and by allowing support from friends or a therapist. One of my top strengths from Positive Psychology is perspective. So I'm continuously processing and reflecting on my own experiences and looking for what I'm learning about myself and how I'm growing through the challenging days.

I have an amazing life, but the fact is there are still days when it feels hard. And I think it's important to acknowledge that. I know I'm usually beaming in my Instagram photos, but trust me, I've had many low moments in my years on this planet.

By opening up to my team about how gutted I felt when I found out yet another friend was struggling to stay alive, I was able to receive the lessons Ali brought forward about seeds and arrows. Those metaphors helped me reframe my work and my purpose. But I wouldn't have learned about them without first feeling safe to open up about my feelings.

Before we can support each other, we have to be responsible for ourselves. Before we can connect with our purpose and our work, we have to connect with ourselves. We are the source of our hope and our devotion. It's inside us. Some days, it's hard to find, but it's there.

Survivor Story

What helped you get through one more day?

I'm a person of faith, so Scripture helped. Psalm 34:18, 'God is close to the brokenhearted and saves those who are crushed in spirit.' And Psalm 73:26, 'My flesh and my heart may fail, but God is the strength of my heart and my portion forever.' I knew God loved me, even when I didn't feel it.

Survivor

A few weeks after writing this section, I had a hard morning. But I know things won't be perfect. I know I have to roll with the punches. In a fight, if you stand stiffly when you're punched, it's going to hurt a lot more. We have to stay flexible, in the flow, ready to adapt. The tools in this book are here to help us roll with the punches, but again and again, we still have to wake up and choose to use them. It can be a practice to find equilibrium again after we're pulled off center, and it's sometimes a struggle.

Right now, I'm on my balcony. I have a ton of work to do, but in this moment, I'm capturing a little peace. A little relief. The sunlight on my body feels good. Being outside and taking a breath of fresh air feels good. I could have sat right down inside at my desk and jumped into research and calls. But I wanted to meet this reality with more peace and compassion. That's a decision only I can make. And I needed space to make it. My friend and shaman Rev. Briana Lynn said to me in my first ayahuasca ceremony: 'When you can breathe, you can choose.' I've remembered this ever since. The simplicity of coming back to our breath and the fact that we're still breathing, and we get to choose in this moment, is so powerful. When you can breathe, you can choose.

Survivor Story

What helped you get through one more day?

One night I came across J. K. Rowling's Harvard commencement speech, and it totally changed everything. I cried until the morning and went down a rabbit hole of self-help books, Positive Psychology and healing, spiritual practices, and therapy. Little by little I changed my whole life. I went from feeding my daughter from a food bank to living my dream.

Survivor

Robert Frost, the poet from New England immortalized for his poem *The Road Not Taken,* is credited with the phrase, 'The best way out is always through.' I think about this phrase a lot when I feel like I don't know how I'm going to get through something. The best way out is through. I have to feel my feelings. I have to take care of myself. And I have to get on with things.

The best way out is through.

The best person to do it is *you.*

Harnessing Hope

I like the idea of harnessing hope. Sure, hope can feel a bit abstract at times, but there's a science to it. The science of hope shows that how we *think* about the future partially shapes the future we'll have. In fact, our optimism level is a good indicator of suicidal risk – the more optimistic you are about your future, the less likely you are to think about ending your life, and increased optimism, hope, and future focus are associated with decreased depressive symptoms and less suicidal behavior.[1] Hope can lead to higher academic achievement, enhanced performance in the workplace, and greater overall happiness.[2] Pretty powerful!

We're not talking about just emptily hoping and wishing for a better day. Rather, *grounded* hope[3] helps build resilience – the capacity to withstand and bounce back – in the face of life's adversities, to help navigate challenging realities by staring them in the face and taking a realistic inventory. Then, you can feel empowered to implement hope strategies and move toward goals for a better future. Some of the many benefits of hope include:

- greater resilience

- improved ability to cope with stress

- reduced anxiety and depression

- experiencing more meaning in life

- overall higher levels of well-being
- higher levels of performance, job satisfaction, and engagement at work
- increased engagement in career exploration
- enhanced creativity
- higher performance goals
- increased motivation
- better academic performance
- more clarity in goal setting

Hope Box

When students join my Mastermind programs, I send out a black gift box with a copy of my book *Now Is Your Chance*, the companion journal, a pen, and a candle to correspond with each of the three sections of the book – body, mind, spirit. Using the Positive Psychology tools in the book, the idea is to create a sensory experience using the candles to support self-connection and journaling when working on happiness. I suggest that my students keep the black gift box and use it as a ritual box, and I invite you to do the same.

Create your own 'Hope Box' – a place to keep your lists, meaningful photos, awe-inspiring items, and other things that boost your levels of hope, devotion, and connection. Make the box a sensory experience by filling it with things that activate your senses. Perhaps your favorite moisturizer or lotion for touch, some beautiful incense for smell, some herbal teabags for taste. Whatever feels good for you. You can bring your Hope Box out each day and use it as a physical anchor to remind you to pick up a Tiny Tool.

Alternatively, you can create a virtual box on your phone – just search for 'Hope Box' in your app store. This works just as well as a physical version. Research shows that using a Hope Box virtually via a smartphone app can increase coping mechanisms for stress, reduce suicidal ideation, and boost perceived reasons to live.[4]

Much of what we know about hope comes from the research of Charles Snyder, who developed Hope Theory – according to his framework, the process of developing strategies for reaching goals is known as *pathways thinking*. Hopeful people have been found to believe there are many pathways to their goals and that none of them are free from obstacles. Flexibility and realism are key features of hope.

OK, so we know there's a whole science around how hope operates. But how do we actually harness hope and put it in motion? Well, there's a step-by-step method you can use to connect your future goals to behaviors and attitudes. It's called a Hope Map. Nice name, right? What a great map to carry with you – one full of hope.

The Hope Map is a tool you can use to set goals, create steps toward achieving them, and design a plan for sustaining your motivation. You'll hear many people talk about self-control and willpower when it comes to achieving goals, but relying solely on these capacities can become exhausting and also ignores this profound source of power and light we are discussing (and learning how to harness) – hope.

The practice of writing about our goals has its own set of benefits. (The ripple effect is everywhere.) It can facilitate the release of emotions, bring awareness and clarity to the things we desire, and give us the chance to reorganize priorities and even reflect on our values. It can also improve self-regulation, help us identify internal conflicts, and discover pathways to resolve them. By writing about our goals, we have an improved likelihood of actually achieving them! Writing therapy is shown to alleviate distress and symptoms of mental health disorders such as post-traumatic stress disorder (PTSD) and depression, as well as support psychological well-being and promote positive dimensions such as forgiveness and gratitude.[5]

Visualizing our best possible future self can lead to incredible, long-lasting results. Specifically, research showed that across four days, 20 minutes per day of writing about their best possible self resulted in participants experiencing better mood and less distress five months later.[6] Five months! Small daily actions really do create big results.

Set a Goal

Write down a goal for today. It could be as simple as getting out of the house for a walk, making your bed, or calling a friend. Here are some questions to guide your writing:

- Which goal feels especially meaningful to you?

- Which goal feels stretchy but still manageable?

- How might this goal connect to your sense of purpose?

- How could you bring flexibility to this goal?

– Can you do a quick reality check about this goal, perhaps considering the time frame or breaking it into smaller goals?

———————————

All right, now we're ready to get to the Hope Map. This is a favorite intervention of mine because you can literally feel it working, and you can use it for any goal – big or small. Practicing hope tools like this will help you get clearer on your goals and what's important to you. You'll be able to develop your creative and strategic thinking and maintain motivation even when faced with challenges.

The Hope Map

Use whatever works best for you to complete this exercise, whether that's a pen and paper, an Excel spreadsheet, or an online mind map.

Step 1: Set your goal

This is a moment for energy and inspiration. What do you want to achieve? Determine a clear and exciting vision of a goal that you'd like to achieve.

Step 2: Identify pathways

Write down several actions, pathways, or steps you can take to pursue the goal.

Step 3: Identify obstacles

What might be standing in the way of reaching your goal? Identify at least one obstacle that might block each of the pathways you've described.

Step 4: Identify pathways to overcome identified obstacles

Moving back to Step 2, review your existing pathways, including strategies to overcome the obstacle identified. Do you need new pathways? Or refinements to your current pathways?

Step 5: What is your goal and 'why?'

Write down why this goal is meaningful to you and how it's aligned with your values. What will happen or how will you feel if you don't achieve this goal?

Step 6: Identify your support system

Do you need support to help you achieve your goal? Where might you find it? Write down your support systems.

Note: Hope Theory teaches that your goals will remain unfulfilled if these six steps aren't completed in this order, so make sure you complete all six of the steps!!

A note about hope

It's important to recognize the limits and dangers of hope. There's research that shows hope is hugely protective against suicide. When people are suicidal, they report feeling hopeless and stuck in their thinking, with an inability to see a way out. It fits then, that boosting levels of hope, which supports more divergent thinking and the ability to reach for multiple pathways and open up cognition, is a protective factor.

However, suppose someone is already demonstrating suicidal behavior. In that case, high levels of hope actually correlate with a higher risk of suicide.[7] This is why prevention is vitally important. Don't wait until you or a loved one are at an edge before you try these tools. Start right now.

Grow through
What You Go through

'In order to feel glorious,
you have to believe you can.'
Ally Love

I remember sitting across from my counselor, two chairs facing each other in a room filled with books, with a small window looking out over the street. She was asking me how I was feeling. I'd shown up to the session as I did every week, not wanting to be there, but knowing I needed to be. Not knowing what to say, but knowing the words would come. Not knowing if I'd ever feel better, but trusting I would. She told me the story of another client who had been on a long journey of recovery, and was feeling better now. As my counselor told the story, it connected me with a feeling of hope and promise. Hearing how this woman had moved forward to live a great life showed me that I could do that too.

Twice in my life, I've worked with therapists to move through symptoms of post-traumatic stress disorder (PTSD). I've navigated various challenges in my journey toward healing. From seeking support from Rape Crisis back in Newcastle, England following a sexual assault to, more recently, getting the results of a brain scan, which guided me to seek support again – each step has been significant. PTSD is a delayed response to a traumatic event which might include symptoms such as disruptive flashbacks, re-triggered distress when re-exposed to a similar situation, or repression and avoidance.[1] PTSD is associated with an increased risk of suicide, with a study of 3.1 million participants in Sweden showing that people diagnosed with PTSD are twice as likely to die by suicide than those without PTSD.[2] This research also showed an average gap of 2.5 years between diagnosis of PTSD and death, which highlights the importance of prevention, and speedy intervention.

A podcast host once asked me the question, 'Niyc, you've been bullied, raped, and lost three close friends to suicide, and you've gone on to be stronger, more successful, and happier than ever before. How?'

Now I know stats like those reported for PTSD above can be illuminating, shocking even. We're painting a picture of a more hopeful future, and I think it's important to know some of the context for the social opportunity we have here to make a change. And why am I happier than ever before? Post-traumatic growth (PTG). PTG is the capacity to grow after adversity. It involves positive psychological changes after trauma or major life challenges, with improvements shown in perspective on life, personal strength, and connection with others, and leads to boosted levels of confidence, appreciation of life, and the willingness to discover new possibilities.[3]

A study of 5,302 US military service members, a population known for high suicide risk, showed that the more PTG service members reported, the lower the incidence of suicidal ideation they reported, too.[4] I want you to know that growth is possible after trauma. You won't just 'get through' or survive, or even 'bounce back' – you have the opportunity to go on to feel better *than ever before*. PTG gives us extra motivation to harness that hope, and keep going for one more day.

Survivor Story

What helped you get through one more day?

At first, I went to see a counselor. I was sexually abused by my dad when I was young, and it took a lot for me to get over it. I couldn't get my questions answered as my dad killed himself when I was 17, before I had the courage to confront him. I was meant to have six counseling sessions but I only went to two. I realized that if I did end my life then the person who made me feel that way would have won. I wasn't going to let him win.

I changed my mindset. At the time I had an online business, so I started watching videos on mindset and thinking of every situation as a positive and never a negative. I'm always kind to people and every situation that they're in. I never look down [on people]... and I take the time to listen to them. All anyone wants is for someone to listen to them.

Survivor

Again, I want to continue to thread through this book that while positive emotions are super important, it's also important to recognize that I'm not overgeneralizing or directing that only positive elements should be focused on. PTG research acknowledges the need for broader frames of reference. It indicates limitations in only taking a positive approach, while also noting that experience of more positive emotions before trauma can help the processing of trauma after it's happened.[5]

A study of those who have lost a loved one to suicide[6] showed that the experience of PTG increased as time passed and was more prevalent in those survivors who sought support, and who had better coping skills, which suggests the application of tools to improve coping and strengthen internal resources, such as the Positive Psychology tools shared in this book, can support growth after trauma. Hold on to the vision that there will be a better day – the research says there will be.

Noticing

One thing I've noticed in myself is that when I'm not feeling good – whether I'm going through a tough day, a health challenge, or I'm simply not feeling as energized as I could – it narrows my thinking and limits my experience of the world. It feels like the walls are closing in on me and I can't think beyond that immediate moment. Simple things like not having enough rest or having too many online meetings scheduled in one day can really impact my energy if I'm not mindful. I've tuned in to the subtleties of what works and doesn't work for me.

Survivor Story

What helped you get through one more day?

I'm rigorous with my daily attention to mindset work and many other healthy habits that help me feel my best.

Survivor

I like to be intentional about expanding my awareness. Here are some simple noticing practices you can try to expand your world a bit on the days you feel you need it.

Noticing Practices

Notice something new

- Go for a walk and keep your phone in your pocket.

- Take deep breaths and look around as you walk.

- Stop to observe any places you typically whizz by.

- Look for something you haven't already seen. Listen for any sounds you don't normally notice.

Typically, we go about our day filtering out a lot of information. Our mind keeps us focused on what's most important based on our past patterning and conditioning. This exercise can interrupt the pattern and start training you to think more mindfully. It's also a tool that's proven to shift you into an energy of manifesting. What's going on in the world around you? Does a neighbor have flowers growing in her front yard? Are there kids laughing as they play together?

When you get home, reflect on your experience.

- What did you notice?

- What surprised you?

- How did the 'noticing walk' affect your mood?

- What did you notice when you came home?

Here are two variations on the Noticing exercise you can try.

Noticing together

1. Sit with a friend and identify three things about each other that you're noticing for the first time.

2. What have you never noticed before? Freckles? Eye color? A pretty piece of jewelry that they always wear?

Share a curiosity

- As you go about your day, make a note of something that seems surprising or makes you curious. It could be a story in the newspaper, a strange sign in the window of a local bookshop, or anything in between.

- Send a text to a friend sharing this curiosity. Invite their thoughts.

Research has shown that mindfulness-based interventions can lead to clinically significant reductions in depression and suicidal ideation.[1] Practicing simple mindfulness techniques can encourage non-emotional observation of suicidal thinking and can help with building self-love and self-kindness. They can also remind you to come back to being present in the moment and living each moment to its fullest.[2]

Survivor Story

What helped you get through one more day?
For me, it was listening to motivation, listening to myself and my thoughts, and figuring out what I needed and what no longer belonged in my life.

Survivor

A New Discovery

Remember Martin Seligman, the 'father of Positive Psychology'? Well, besides everything else I've learned from him, I had chills when I read his book *The Hope Circuit*, which shares the outcome of an experiment he and Steve Maier led which completely turned Seligman's earlier famous 'learned helplessness' research on its head.

What was it specifically that gave me chills? It was when Seligman recounted the story of waking up in the early hours of the morning with total clarity that he'd identified 'The Hope Circuit'.

Wow – a circuit that shows us that future bad events will be controllable, which will buffer us against helplessness and anxiety.

What does it mean? It means that depression and anxiety in humans will soon become curable via this pathway. How can we not feel hopeful reading that?

Choose Your Own Adventure

As we're moving through *One More Day*, let's think about this journey as carving our new path. Weaving the tools through your life. Choosing your own adventure. When you consider your mental health journey as an *adventure,* how does it feel? Lighter? Less of a burden or a hassle? The fun part is you get to decide how you want to integrate these tools, so they work best for you.

Do you love structure and organization? Then you may like to have these Positive Psychology tools scheduled in your day. Perhaps you'll start with 10 minutes of breathing. After lunch you can take a walk. Evening might work best for your journaling practice. Maybe sticking to the same routines every day at the same times will help you stay on track – stay on a hopeful path.

However, sometimes when you're struggling, sticking to a plan may feel like a lot. I know that having people tell you to stick to a routine can make you feel even worse. In that case, maybe taking a more go-with-the-flow approach is better. I know I've benefited from having more space and fluidity in my days recently. Allow yourself that opportunity. Tap into what your body tells you. I'm a big fan of listening to your body, feeling the pang of intuition, and letting it guide you.

What feels light to you? What feels heavy or hard? What feels good? Look back over the Tiny Tools list. What calls out to you, right now? Choose that. What do you need to have a good day today?

Experiment. Get curious. Try different methods. Maybe have one week with a mapped-out routine, and another where you let yourself choose in the moment where you want to put your energy. When it comes to work habits, allow in that spirit of experimentation as well. Can you create ideas on a walk? As I've written in other sections, I've been enjoying this method so much. Does music help you focus? Does a morning workout help you feel vibrant throughout the day, or does it help more to look forward to a power hour at the gym after work?

When it comes to your mental health journey, you can choose your own adventure. You can be an explorer! No matter how terrible you may feel, there's still so much out there in the world for you to discover. We're always learning and growing. What a magical idea. Better days have to be out there, because we're expanding as well as figuring out how to establish routines that will help us have better days more consistently.

The Power of Positive Environments

One of the key frameworks in Positive Psychology is the PERMA criteria of flourishing, which teaches that Positive Emotions, Engagement, Relationships, Meaning, and Accomplishment are all required to build a flourishing self and life. The science recently expanded upon this PERMA criteria for flourishing to also include mindset, finance, health, and environments – PERMA+4. [1] I want to focus here on how positive environments can help interrupt negative patterns and shift thinking from suicide to hope.

Throughout the writing of *One More Day*, I've had countless conversations that have surprised me. It really has astounded me just how many people's lives have been touched by suicide. I've always said this book is an opportunity to create more conversations about suicide prevention, and I really experienced that when people started to open up.

As well as hearing many stories from friends and people I'd met in person, I also shared an online survey to learn more from others who had experienced suicidal thinking in the past. What I was most curious about is what compelled them to stay alive in the precise moment they were going to quit. What was it that made them want to live? The results were fascinating.

Survivor Story

What helped you get through one more day?

I changed my external environment and worked deep within because I knew there were inner child wounds that were making me feel like a failure. I realized that life was for living not existing and plunged into self-help books and videos and got a coach.

Survivor

One survivor describes how a change in environment along with more intentional eating have had a positive impact.

> I bought a static lodge by a lake where I can sit and reflect every day and be surrounded by nature. I changed my food choices and reduced processed foods to have a clearer brain and less pain.

Another survivor's life underwent a major shift when she and her husband decided to move. In her words:

> My husband and I had agreed that something BIG had to change in our lives in order for me to get better. We'd battled long enough and weren't getting anywhere, the meds were getting increased, and I wasn't getting any better. I'd tried many versions of counseling, but they didn't seem to resonate or work. I tried to reduce my hours at work, but the role wouldn't allow for anything less. So, we decided to emigrate and moved to Cyprus, where work/life and family have a far better balance. We work to live here and not vice versa. I didn't heal overnight but the sunshine, being with my family more, better diet and having distance from unhealthy relationships meant I was starting to feel a lot more like myself.

Nature-based solutions

There's nothing quite like feeling the exhale when I get into the ocean, or I take in the view on a hike. Nature fills us up! Nature-based therapy is made up of six categories: stimulation, acceptance, purification, insight, recharging, and change.[2] Nature can provide us with increased positive emotions; a sense of relaxation, comfort, and awe; and the ability to connect more clearly with thoughts and experience insights. It's also a free form of therapy that we can access just by getting outside into natural environments.

We can also consider the changes we might be able to make so we can nourish ourselves more in our own indoor environments, such as creating cozy spaces in our home. Decluttering your environment is a great place to start, and while it's good to maximize natural light exposure in the daytime, you can use lower, warmer lighting indoors in the evening to support your circadian rhythms. Weighted blankets have been shown to improve sleep and reduce anxiety, and listening to nature sounds, mantras, sound frequencies, or white noise can help relaxation.

Micro Moves

As I approached this section of the book, my mind flashed back to an intensely challenging time when I was struggling with mold poisoning and the brain fog that came with it. It was a time when suicidal thinking had touched me again. High levels of stress in my body had aggravated the mold poisoning, and I had symptoms of anxiety, depression, ADHD, PTSD, and a hormone imbalance.

It was an effort just to make it through a few hours of the day. Never mind thinking about goals, growing my business, or writing another book. Every ounce of energy I had, I used just to try to keep myself functioning. I'd summon everything I had for one coaching call, to keep showing up for my students.

Earlier, we learned we can reach for our Tiny Tools in challenging moments. You can also incorporate them into your daily life to build your resilience muscle and help you become more centered, positive, and productive – like plugging yourself in, getting your battery charged.

But sometimes even reaching for a Tiny Tool feels overwhelming. At those times, you need something even tinier than a Tiny Tool. Enter Micro Moves – a list of low-effort, high-reward, and accessible actions that will help to shift your physical and/or emotional state in a positive way. Here are some ideas of micro moves you can make:

- Take three deep breaths. Now.

- Sigh as you exhale.

- Think of one thing you're grateful for.

- Drink a glass of water.

- Lay on your back. Point your toes then release. Press your heels into the floor as you do this, so you rock your body up and down each time you point and flex your feet. Do this for 60 seconds.

- Lay on one side with your knees bent. Gently rock back and forth for 60 seconds. Repeat on the other side.

- Celebrate yourself for making a micro move.

I feel good most days now because I practice these things daily. It's a lifestyle, not a chore. Life can still come and kick me in the ass. When it does, I come back to my Tiny Tools. And if even the Tiny Tools are too much in the moment, I come back to the Micro Moves. They help me shift toward lightness.

Raising Our Voices

In the US, 50,000 people died by suicide in 2023, more than any other year on record. It's the second leading cause of death among young people, with suicide rates having increased 52.2 percent between 2000 and 2021 in the 10–24 age range, in the US. This figure doesn't include suicide attempts, which are up to 20 times more frequent than completed suicide. Worldwide, we lose over 700,000 people a year to suicide, a statistic which has increased since COVID meant more people experienced the acute effects of the pandemic and lockdowns, as well as the unanticipated fallout of isolation and loneliness, with many still suffering from mental health challenges, job losses, or other financial upsets.[1] We're now experiencing a collective call to wake up and start looking after ourselves, each other, and our world.

Suicide is more common in rural areas and some groups, such as Veterans, Indigenous people, and LGBTQ+ youth, are at greater risk. In the US, suicide rates are highest among Indigenous populations; however, the rising rates of suicide among young people and particularly among young African Americans have also become a public health crisis. The Center for Disease Control and Prevention (CDC) found that among teen girls, a third considered a suicide attempt, and one in seven boys had considered the same.[2] Suicide rates among African American children are accelerating the most rapidly of any group. African

American children between five and 12 are twice as likely as white children in the US to die by suicide.[3] At the same time, African Americans are less likely to receive treatment for depression, with a report showing that only 25 percent of African Americans sought treatment for mental health, compared with 40 percent of white Americans.[4] Unequal access to health care and prejudice from health care providers are reported as contributing factors to these statistics.

The American Academy of Child & Adolescent Psychiatry identifies some obstacles to treating this high-risk population. 'Mental health and substance use problems occurring in Black youth are often under recognized, under treated, or misdiagnosed due in part to bias, discrimination, and structural racism.'[5] Inequities in funding for research further compound the problem, with research led by people of color being less likely to receive funding at the institutional level.

I want to highlight a crisis among young females of color, especially evident in the CDC's 2019 Youth Risk Behavior Survey. It revealed alarming rates of suicide attempts among Black (15 percent), Hispanic (12 percent), and white (9 percent) female high school students. Hispanic youth are 30 percent more likely to attempt suicide and Black girls are 1.7 times more likely to attempt suicide than their white counterparts. Coupled with the fact that Hispanics are 50 percent less likely to receive mental health treatment, and only 4 percent of psychologists and 2 percent of psychiatrists are Black, the systemic nature of this issue is clear.

I remember both how scared I was to ask for help as an 11-year-old struggling with suicidal thinking and the immense fear I felt when I was being bullied. For young Black girls, there's an added layer of unsafety when faced with the prospect of talking to a therapist who doesn't look like them. As well as us all doing the work to talk more and make it OK to share how we're feeling, we must continue to work on the systems and structures that facilitate the provision of support and take an honest look at the vast gap that needs to be closed when it comes to delivering mental health interventions in a way that's accessible for all.[6]

No one, particularly high-risk groups, should be left feeling stuck somewhere they don't feel safe. I know my privilege means I'll never fully understand the nuances of the struggle in the detail I wish I could. But I can be an ally. I can show up. I can try my best to learn, ask questions, and integrate what I'm learning. I can do my best, and we can all do better.

We have to be intentional in thinking about the contexts that lead to these troubling figures – the intersectional disparities across education, housing, health care – and we must recognize that the challenges of righting things are complex, in part because hundreds of years of inequality mean it's not a level playing field we're operating on.[7] 1.7 times more likely to take one's own life. We have to open our eyes to the fact that just because you may not treat someone differently based on their race that doesn't mean you don't have an advantage or privilege.

Another major social determinant of mental health is financial hardship, which is one of the single strongest socio-economic predictors of poor mental health. Financial struggle is cited as a common reason for suicidal thinking and behaviors. Factors that can buffer the effect include ethnic self-identity, how financial hardship is perceived subjectively, and hope. Having a sense of agency and empowerment matters.

Speaking up

We must be mindful that everyone is fighting a different version of the battle. We don't often know the full complexity or context. Just like with our well-being, there isn't a point where we'll have it all figured out. We're not going to arrive at a time where this is behind us, because it'll always be shaping what happens now. But in 2021, a massive 94 percent of Americans surveyed said they thought suicide can be prevented. It can.

I know we need to do more at a policy and organizational level to make sure changes are being put into place to give a chance to people who haven't previously had access. Within my journey of learning more about racism and systemic inequality, I educate myself by reading books and journal articles, and paying for courses, and I try not to put questions to my friends of color, unless invited to do so. They're already dealing with the impact of racism and social injustice every day and they share that it's exhausting and painful. They feel the longstanding toll of prejudice.

I saw a clip of my friend Elliott speaking on stage about the needs of young Black people. He shared that he'd read a textbook in grad school about the culture in psychotherapy, which stated that Black people don't care about their mental health. He went on to encourage more openness about mental health, more permission to listen, more vulnerability, and the willingness to be uncomfortable and talk about the issue in the context of self-love, increased awareness of our own brilliance, and an understanding of where we've come from. It's up to me, and us all, to do the research to improve mental health outcomes for those groups whose lives aren't as valued in our society.

I spoke with my friend, author, and transformational soul coach Rha Goddess about this topic for guidance. Here is what she said:

We have to back all the way up to think about how systems and structures operate to create insecurity in the hearts, minds, and spirits of all people. Let's begin there. From many years of supporting young women in dire circumstances, I'll tell you that what has been someone's marketing campaign has become someone else's psychological hell. Whether we look at the conversation of beauty, or sexuality, or who has permission to be expressed versus who doesn't, or who gets to raise their voice to show anger and who doesn't, we get messaging every single step of the way that people of color – and specifically, Black women – don't matter. What does that do to one's psyche? When at every turn, baked into every system and structure, you've received every message of 'you don't matter' you can possibly receive? There's a continual need for a struggle and a fight for Black women. You're exhausted before you even leave the house.

I'm surprised that figure [on the higher likelihood of Black girls to attempt suicide than their white counterparts] isn't higher. In some ways it speaks to our resilience, but it shows up in other statistics like substance abuse, abusive relationships, the way we sit down on our potential and don't believe we're worthy or deserving. A young girl who hates her skin may not physically take her own life, but she may put herself in circumstances where her life is in jeopardy, where her health is in jeopardy, her freedom is in jeopardy, over and over again.

What is it in our psychology that tells us that some lives are more important than others? The way this has been normalized should be frightening to everyone. We've got to be more vigilant about understanding the nature of the messages we're sending. If little Black girls feel that the color of their skin is a curse, we have to ask ourselves, what have we done to create that? We're operating out of our own unhealed trauma and dysfunction. So, the solution begins with us being willing to no longer tolerate the state of our world. To no longer tolerate the kinds of messages in the name of bubblegum or blue jeans that dictate who the pretty girls are. Or that dictate who is worthy to be listened to or who deserves safety.

The more that we as everyday people become adamant about the fact that this is intolerable, the more systems and structures will have to bend and shift and change. We're waiting for some message on high to trickle down and topple our systems, but change has always come from the ground up. The people have always led, not the leaders.

It's gonna be up to us to sort of decide who we want to be. Where do I have an opportunity in my immediate circle? We all have a role to play in how we demonstrate our lack of tolerance for those things that we know are feeding the dynamic. What needs to be cultivated?

Rha reminds us that we're all powerful. We're not powerless. Each and every one of us can do something. Have you thought about what role you'd like to play? What opportunity you can find? What can you cultivate?

These words echoed the message of connection I've been talking about throughout this book. Rha recognizes that sometimes we're afraid to overstep boundaries, but we do have to practice taking an extra step. She goes on to say: 'Sometimes it's just a hug. Letting them know you see them, you care – *that* can be the revolution.'

Awesomeness

Awe. What comes to mind when you read that word? You might think of the Grand Canyon. A waterfall. An opera by Mozart. Perhaps the Taj Mahal or Michelangelo's painted ceiling in the Sistine Chapel.

Awe is that feeling of heart-bursting, gasp-inducing WOW that happens when you feel the massiveness of something that positively captures your attention. It could be the feeling of awe when you see a beautiful view, when you witness an act of kindness between two people, when you listen to music that you feel within your soul. And if you're anything like me, when you receive a text with the fireworks effect on your phone!

Having more experiences of awe has an incredible range of benefits for your physical and mental health, including:

- increased levels of the bonding hormone oxytocin
- increased prosocial behaviors and social integration
- increased sense of meaning and diminished focus on the self
- lowered heart rate, along with reductions in inflammation, autoimmune issues, and sympathetic nervous system arousal (meaning fight or flight isn't as readily activated)
- reduction in symptoms of stress, anxiety, depression, pain, and suicidal ideation and behaviors[1]

Wow. All from experiencing more awe! You might think that you're powerless to create more awe in your life if you don't live right by Niagara Falls. But it turns out, we all have the power to bring awe into our lives. More awe can be created by engaging in inspiring conversations, philosophizing over a big idea, investing time in nature, even looking at images of nature online.

When you engage with awe-inspiring experiences you become more generous, cooperative, more willing to sacrifice for other people, less entitled, and more likely to share.

I remember my soul sister Koya introducing me to her friend Mani, who founded a well-being-based VR company called TRIPP. I tried out the well-being program, which took you (virtually) into Ram Dass's office space. Immediately I felt a powerful, expansive feeling of awe as I experienced the surroundings within the VR headset.

Here's a couple of *awe*some interventions for you to try.

Awe Intervention

- Find photos of places or things which look impressive to you and make you feel a sense of awe. Anything that activates the feeling of 'wow!'

- Create a photo album on your phone labeled 'AWEsome!' and save your awe-inspiring photos in there.

- Add the photos to your Hope Box (*see page 38*) so you can bring it out whenever you need a boost and activate the feeling of awe and the benefits associated with it.

Awe Walk

Head out on a walk and look out for any awesome things you might see. You may not come across a Wonder of the World, but you might find some mini awe-inspiring sights. (As you know by now, I'm all for keeping things simple.) Here are some ideas to get you started:

- sunrise/sunset
- a pretty shell
- a butterfly
- a waterfall
- a hummingbird
- a family laughing together
- changing colors of the season
- light shining between the leaves on the trees
- the sky's reflection in a lake

Awe walks have been shown to enhance well-being. The key element is turning the attention outward, creating a reduced focus on the self.

Another way to explore awe is through dance, chants, prayers, and celebration. I remember my friend Natalie creating the most amazing fire dance experience for us in South Africa where we got to participate in a local ritual as a group. It felt so special and powerfully activating to dance in the darkness with the fire as our light.

As I was writing this section of the book, I felt ready to take a break and wanted to move my body. I opted for a hike because I wanted to get into nature. As soon as I was outside, I started feeling the awesome benefits. What could you do to bring more 'awe' or 'mini awe' into your life?

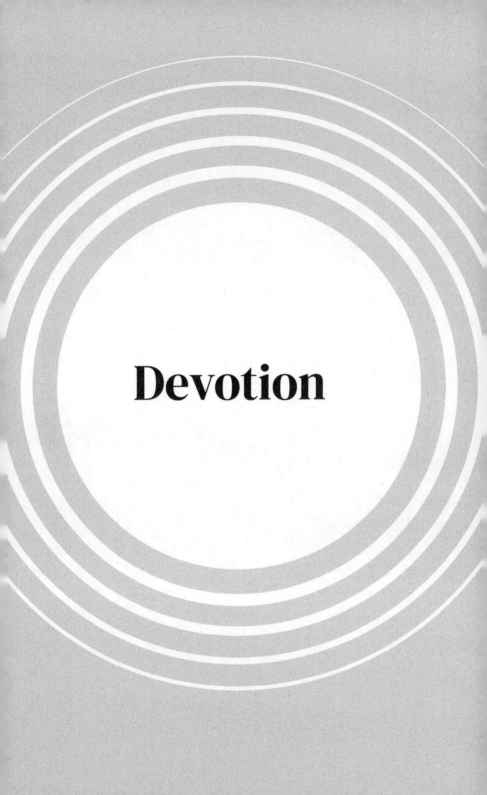

Devotion

Drawing on
Your Strengths

In my first book, I talked about doing what you do best by putting your strengths to work.

If celebrating and working toward your strengths can help you thrive, you're certainly going to want to rely on them when you're going through tough times or helping others who are having a hard time themselves.

The science of Positive Psychology was built upon the foundational understanding of character strengths. It teaches that we all have 24 measurable character strengths, grouped into six categories of virtues, which help us become stronger and more successful when identified and intentionally used. Character strengths are associated with low levels of suicide ideation in older adults and are a protective factor against behavioral problems in adolescents. Strengths also activate hope. When you know for certain you're good at something, and you have strengths – which everybody does – your level of hopefulness can improve because of that.[1] Your self-esteem increases, and you can find more will to live.

Suicide prevention research shows that peer leaders trained in strengths in schools were four times more likely to refer a suicidal friend to an adult.[2] It also shows that using a physical card deck when working with strengths can help – the cards are tangible and can increase mindfulness and presence, to avoid getting stuck in overthinking. The strengths that are firmly proven in the science to protect against suicidal ideation and behavior include gratitude, love, and engagement.

You're good at things. You're strong. And it's OK to speak up and ask for help.

Survivor Story

What helped you get through one more day?

Asking for help when I needed it, letting go of fear and shame, surrounding myself with the best people, taking a break when I had too much on my plate, and introducing happiness hobbies gradually again.

Survivor

Have you ever done an assessment to determine your strengths? The VIA Character Strengths Survey is one I recommend.

When researching this book, I found an interesting statistic that there's one death by suicide every 40 seconds – but there's one person taking the VIA Character Strengths test every 15 seconds.[3] As well as this, I shared earlier that 135 people are impacted by each suicide. Well, the same number of people – 135 – are impacted by the ripple effect of Positive Psychology. I have chills writing this and I wish for a better day when having generated enough energy through discovering our strengths and practicing Positive Psychology tools, we can activate the compound effect and deepen the social strength sufficiently to prevent suicide.

Survivor Story

What helped you get through one more day?

I immersed myself in female business groups. I learned about meditation, read Louise Hay, listened to hundreds of inspirational audiobooks. I learned Reiki, sound therapy, and became a meditation leader. I found that Positive Psychology was real and began to weave it into my life.

Survivor

I'm approaching this book the way Positive Psychology approaches mental wellness. Instead of focusing on what's going wrong, I want to focus on what's going right. I want to bring attention to the stories of those who overcame thoughts of taking their own lives and came out the other side. The subject is heavy, but I know from my own expertise and experience that we can make more progress when we approach it from a positive angle.

Reflection

Pull out your journal or the notes section on your phone and think about the unique abilities YOU bring to the world.

– What do you see as your strengths?

– What do others see as your strengths? (You may have to ask them!)

– What helps you feel productive? (You can interpret this question any way you want. Perhaps you'd like to think about what conditions are most suitable for work, or what lifestyle routines are most supportive.)

– How do you like to energize your day and have more positivity in it?

Identifying your strengths

Have you ever felt like you're dragging yourself through your day task by task? Me too. And it's not always because you're too tired, although that can often be what you put it down to.

The fact is what you direct your attention to in your day does matter. And there are some activities that will give you energy and some that will take it away. Determining which activities are going to help you feel good all comes down to the application of your personal strengths.

If you haven't already taken the VIA Character Strengths Survey, put down this book and do it now! It's proven that just finding out what your strengths are boosts your well-being. Just finding out! Once you know what your strengths are, you're able to apply them to your day. But first we want to take stock of what's working and not working right now, so we can identify where you can improve things.

A strength identifies your preexisting capacity for a way of thinking, feeling, or behaving that feels true to you, is energy-giving, and enables optimal functioning and performance.[4] Think about the days when you're tired AF. You'd give anything to feel clear-headed and energized.

When you choose activities that use your strengths, you enjoy them more and they raise your energy levels. On the flip side, doing things you're not good at is going to drain you. That's proven in the science, too, which shows that weaknesses lead to disengagement, negative feelings, and a lack of motivation.[5]

The good news is: We're all good at something! But you have to take the test to find out what that is. So, if you ignored me above and just read on, put down the book (for a minute) and go do the test now.

Did you take it? Wonderful. I love it! OK. What are your strengths? I like to write mine down and keep them within arm's reach so I can give myself a little pep talk whenever I need it. They're literally written on a giant Post-it note and stuck on my office wall!

Find Your Red and Green Activities

This exercise will help you get mindful over the things that energize you and the things that drain you. We're going to define what 'red' and 'green' activities are, and then we're going to take a close look at your day and rate your activities using an energy scale. Then we'll figure out how to get more energizing moments into your day and remove as many energy-depleting ones as possible. First, let's define them.

Green activities:

– use your strengths and give you energy

– are things you enjoy doing

– make you feel energized

– lead to a sensation that time passes by unnoticed

– are things you look forward to doing

– are things you can do well, even if you feel stressed or tired

Red activities:

– rely on your weaknesses and deplete your energy

– are things you don't like doing

- make you feel drained

- lead to the sensation of time passing slowly

- are things you don't look forward to

- require a lot of effort, focus, and self-control to do well

Let's take a look at your red and green activities.

Step 1

Record your red and green moments by providing a description of the activity and the energy levels you felt while engaged in the activity.

Rate each activity using the following scale:

- −2 = required a lot of energy

- −1 = required some energy

- 0 = neutral (didn't give or take energy)

- +1 = gave you positive energy

- +2 = gave you a lot of positive energy

Use a table like this to track your scores:

Green Activities	Energy +/–	Notes
Red Activities	Energy +/–	Notes

At the end of the day, highlight your most energy-giving and energy-depleting activities. Repeat Step 1 every day for a week.

I know doing something for seven days might feel like a lot, but at the end of the week you'll have a really robust insight into the things that bring you energy. And even if you just complete today, that's progress, and you did enough to see what feels good for you.

Step 2

Select the top 3–5 activities that give you the most energy and the top 3–5 activities that deplete your energy.

Step 3

Take out your journal or notes section on your phone and reflect on the following questions:

– What did you discover from this exercise?

– How can you include more green activities in your week so you can use your strengths more often?

– How can you improve your experience of the activities that deplete your energy?

– Could you delete them? (Stop doing them.)

– Could you delegate them? (Give the activities to somebody else to do.)

– Could you shift your mindset around them? (E.g. set a timer and make it a fun challenge to get it done.)

- Could you load up some green activities before you tackle a red activity, so you have momentum to carry through the task you don't want to do?

So how do strengths apply to mental health, specifically?

Let's keep it simple here... EVERYBODY is good at something. We ALL have the same palette of strengths – we just use them in different ways, and we have different combinations of top strengths too. It's really refreshing to know this. Even on your hardest day, in your darkest hour, you still have your strengths! And what's more, your strengths give you energy. When I've had low moments – or honestly, entire months where I've felt like I'm underwater with a cloud permanently hanging over me and I just can't catch a break – I remember I have strengths, and that they give me energy when I use them. The simple act of remembering these two things is enough to motivate me to look at my list of strengths. I actually think the notes section of my phone is a Positive Psychology intervention in itself at this stage! I store my strengths list in there, too. I'll add bullet points and check off ways I've tested and played with using my strengths.

What next?

I remember finding out what my strengths were, but then having an enormous gap in my mind about how to actually use them.

When I was struggling and trying to keep up some semblance of a normal personal and professional life, I reminded myself of the power of using my strengths to help get me through. One of my top strengths is 'maximizer,' which focuses on helping others create excellence, and helping transform things that are strong to be superb. When I remember I can use my maximizer strength to facilitate change and support my students, it gets me excited about the impact I can have. Instead of approaching a Zoom call as just another Zoom call I have to get through, now I have a fun, energizing way to use my strengths!

Once you've taken the assessment and you know what your top strengths are, I want you to try this tool so you can take the next step.

Daily Exceptions Journal

This tool was developed by the clinical psychologist Fredrike Bannink. It helps boost your feelings of competence and control to choose to do more of what works to change your situation for the better.[6] The Daily Exceptions Journal asks you to track how you positively deal with a problem every day for a week. This encourages solution-based thinking and helps raise awareness about what you're doing right when managing particular problems, and which of your strengths you're using to do that.

In your Daily Exceptions Journal, you're invited to record when a problem *doesn't* occur and why. This helps identify existing coping mechanisms, and what's already working, so in the future you can reach for these strategies and build up resilience as a result.

Instructions

Every day this week, answer the following 10 questions:

1. What has improved today, even if it's just a little bit?

2. What else has improved?

3. What did I do differently to improve things?

4. What did I think or believe about myself that was helpful to make these improvements? What was different?

5. When didn't I experience the problem today?

6. What happens when the problem begins to resolve itself? What am I doing to bring this resolution about?

7. When was the problem less of a problem today?

8. What could I do to continue to make improvements?

9. What would my life look like if things continued to improve?

10. What can I congratulate myself for today?

Through reviewing your Daily Exceptions Journal, you can notice strengths like continued persistence, self-kindness, humor, asking for help, finding meaning, or looking after basic needs like sleep. As well as being energizing and engaging, strengths help you harness hope and activate behavior change for lasting results.

I love this intervention! It's so easy to get stuck in the loop of thinking about what isn't working and what's going wrong – this practice asks better questions so you can start to focus on what's going right.

The Bliss of Lists

I have a list for everything. Not just a list – a checklist. Here's a sneak peek:

- To-do list
- To-do today list
- Tiny Tools list
- 'Done' list
- Manifestation list
- Gratitude list
- Awesome-things-about-me list
- Daily-plan list
- Abundance-flowing-in list
- To-pay list
- To-buy list
- Travel list (lots of emojis on this one)
- To-dabble-in list
- Joy list
- Bucket list

Making lists can help create clarity on your goals, keep you on track toward them, and relieve some of the burden of thinking about making a plan.[1]

Creating Space
for Yourself

Connection is a core value of mine, and I know that relationships are the real riches in life. Some days I have so much on my plate with my businesses, writing, and all of the normal life things, and I need to prioritize, which means I draw boundaries around my time. Without a laser focus on my priorities, I won't be able to reach my goals and take care of the important things in my life, including my mental health.

Recently, my friends asked me to join them at one of our favorite lunch spots. I'm a sucker for the salads there, and I love catching up together. I was so grateful for the invite – and I was hungry – so I joined them but kept it short. They asked me to keep hanging out, and I said no, I needed to get back. It wasn't that I wanted to dive right back into work. Instead, I needed time to rest in my own energy.

Do you take time to rest in your energy? Do you give yourself space between working, appointments, and social events? I've learned over the years that I need space to allow inspired ideas to come through. If I fill the calendar up with activities, whether work-related, health-related, or social, I won't have the in-between space I need. And believe me, this is still very much a practice! I began scheduling gray space on my calendar where I do nothing.

That's right, nothing. I just roam around the house and think. Gavin, the therapist I was working with, called it 'Grace Space,' which I absolutely loved and adopted too. In the event in my calendar, I added into the notes a reminder that this Grace Space allowed me to use my strength of intellection, too, so I garnered even more enjoyment from the time to process.

After that lunch was over, I probably had to repeat 10 times that I wasn't going to spend a long time hanging around to chat. I knew there would be pushback and that it was up to me to hold on to the plan that would support my highest growth. *Are you sure you don't want to stay and have a glass of wine, Niyc? Do you not just want to come to the next place? Come on, there's a party later.*

Again and again, I said no, I was heading home. It became comical. I started laughing on my way out. 'Shut the fuck up. I'm not coming!' I finally said, but not in an angry way. I can deliver a phrase like that with playfulness and humor because I know my people really well. People know my heart is good and my intention is pure. They know, even when I'm challenging them, that I'm holding a loving context and container. Maybe swearing isn't your thing. Communicate in whatever way feels good for you. We all have different ways of saying no. And remember that 'No' is a complete sentence all on its own.

Whenever I get an invite, I tune in to how it feels in my body first. I get a flash of intuition that tells me whether I'm a 'yes' for the thing or not. I can also logically ask myself some clarifying questions, such as: *Is this going to support my healing journey right now? Does this align with my big initiatives for who I'm becoming this year? Are fun and laughter what I really need right now?* Because believe me, there have been many times when I've felt resistant to leaving the house, but my friends have encouraged me to do so, and it's helped me feel a million times better when I did. Sometimes, doing something just for fun can also support your highest productivity and growth. Making it a priority to get to know yourself and your patterns can help you tune in to what you really need for you right now.

Survivor Story

What helped you get through one more day?

At first medication and therapy helped. Now I'm protective of my time and make sure I exercise every day.

Survivor

In *The Four Agreements* (one of my favorite books), Don Miguel Ruiz tells us, 'We have learned to live by other people's points of view because of the fear of not being accepted and of not being good enough for someone else.' So, it takes practice to change the question we ask ourselves from '*Will this keep people happy?*' to '*Does this align with my goals?*'

After lunch that day, I received a message from one of my friends who'd been at the restaurant. 'Niyc,' she said, 'I wish I'd left as well.' This friend had a different reason for wishing she'd drawn a boundary. She went on to explain that things took a turn after I'd left. 'I felt like the energy and the conversation were super negative.' When you start to curate your environment to be more supportive of your positive mental health journey, you realize you want to be surrounded by constructive energy and things that feel good.

If you want to feel better in yourself, your day, and your life, look at the quality of the conversations you're having. Are you gossiping? Are you stuck talking about problems in your lives all the time? Are you fixating on everything going wrong in the world? Or are you talking about possibility and opportunity? Are you lifting each other up? Supporting each other's ideas? Encouraging a growth mindset? If you want to know the quality of your life, know the quality of your relationships. Asking questions like these will help you get clear on which social plans are supportive and which might be draining. It can be a really simple shift, and it's going to make you feel better, too.

It's important to be intentional about where we put our energy. Are you allowing yourself to be dragged down or choosing to put yourself in environments where you can be lifted up?

Reminder: You're already doing an awesome thing working on yourself by reading this book. Bravo!

It's important to get clear and committed on what you've decided is best for you. If I don't know how I want to spend my day and my week, then when someone asks me to come to lunch, I won't have any way of evaluating whether it's a good use of my time.

If you've decided you're taking the next 30 days to work on your mental health and your ability to support someone else who's struggling, that's your purpose. You commit to it and then ask: What are the conditions I need to create a mental health plan that will help me realize that goal? What does my day look like? What does my week look like? What could throw me off? Perhaps you want to work through a chapter of this book each week. Or maybe you want to commit to doing a hike once per week and dinner with a friend each weekend. These plans are the practical side of your devotion and are an indicator that you're practicing devotion to yourself.

Let's break down this idea with the example of working through *One More Day*. What's your goal when it comes to this book you're holding? Do you want to get cozy in your house and read it all at once? Do you want to read 10 pages a day as part of your Tiny Tools list and work through the exercises as you go? Maybe you want to gather with friends and make it into a little book club with built-in accountability partners for working through the prompts and exercises.

Do whatever you need. Whatever feels good.

Now, consider what obstacles you might meet. Maybe work will spill over into the evenings. Maybe friends will be in town, wanting you to go out. Boundaries can be subtle, and enforcing them can be done gently, too. Come up with a plan for gently and clearly reinforcing your boundaries. How will you communicate your priorities?

Here are a few ways I managed this and some phrases I practiced saying:

- 'Right now, I'm giving myself a lot more space to look after myself. It's important to me, and it's feeling good to do that. I won't make it, but thank you for inviting me.'

- 'I'd absolutely love to come another time. This time, I can't make it because I'm prioritizing my mental health.'

- 'I can't make it this time. Please invite me next time, and I'll tell you when I'm able to make it.'

- 'I'm looking after myself and focusing on self-care right now. Having no plans on my calendar is really helping. Thank you so much for supporting me and for understanding I can't make it.'

- 'I appreciate you inviting me. I have a lot going on right now. I'd love to get together one-on-one next week rather than in a big group so we can really connect.'

Practice responding when someone asks you to do something, and you really need the time for yourself. Can you let them know one of your biggest priorities right now is engaging in your mental health plan? Can you ask for their support? Can you state clearly that you're not coming or that you'll leave early? Can you share why your positive mental health plan is a non-negotiable for you?

This last question brings us to meaning and purpose and, if others support you or are interested in this work, perhaps another path to building community.

I've learned over the past year especially to get clearer and clearer with friends and loved ones. Orit, one of my close friends, is the most epic social coordinator. She'd been asking me to join in with some events, and I hadn't been able to make it work. I felt called to leave her a voice note to share some of the hard stuff that was going on. I said, 'I just want to share what's going on. I don't want you to think I'm complaining or getting stuck in the negative. I just want to tell you about what's going wrong, so you know I'm not just ghosting on all of our plans. I feel really good about my work, which is going really well. Everything is moving forward, and the bad things are working their way out. I appreciate your support.'

Orit responded and told me there was no need to apologize and that she was there for me. And she gave me some really encouraging words: 'You're amazing. I'm so proud of you for focusing. You never have any problem from me. I'm just selfish and want to spend time with you!'

Clear communication. What a blessing, right? I always find when I communicate more clearly, my friends receive it more clearly. The energy feels much better.

Survivor Story

What helped you get through one more day?

I focused on keeping my world very small, reduced any pressures on me, and gave myself permission to do nothing unless I wanted to. I was supported by my husband and sister who listened, accepted, and protected me.

My approach to how I led my life shifted. Initially it was hard work and exhausting, now it's natural, and I'm so in tune with my own emotions. I listen to what my emotions are telling me and use this to guide me.

Survivor

When we're clear about our priorities to ourselves, then we can be clear about them to others. The boundaries follow naturally. It's not that we're saying 'no' to someone else's idea. It's that we're committed to our own goals. We're devoted. Our empowerment will come through communication.

One Thing

Water the plants.

For me, this was another item on my to-do list, along with taking out the trash and folding laundry. They're not problems at all. Nor are they even life hassles. But honestly, when you're struggling with the way you feel, having a list of things to do can feel so heavy. I noticed the subtle energy drain I was feeling for having all these little things I'd put on my own plate.

For one of my friends, gardening is therapy. He'd show me photos of how his garden was growing and it gave me perspective because for a while, the same kind of activity was still a chore for me. *Remember to water the plants. Oh no, forgot to water the plants. Ugh!*

I remember telling another friend, Will, 'I need to get someone to come water the plants.' He looked me straight in the eyes with a confused look on his face and said, 'Can't you just water your own plants, Niyc?' It was in that moment of simple challenge that I realized – of course I can just water my plants. Mic-drop moment! It felt like an exhale, and it was the tiniest, simplest, most uneventful reframe inside my mind which shifted my perspective.

Will's question reminded me of the topic of reframing. When you feel like you're underwater and you're having hard days, your working memory is impacted, and it's hard to remember the little things, like where you put your keys, never mind have the awareness of your thinking patterns and how to get more done.

What if I applied a different frame to watering my plants? What if I treated this as a Positive Psychology mindfulness-based intervention? What if I filled the watering can cheerfully, and poured the water mindfully? Focused on that one thing, perhaps even summoning gratitude for getting to breathe in the fresh, clean air these plants bring us, to watch them grow and change through the seasons? Giving life to something within my home.

What if I chose my plants to be my therapy too?

So I did.

And now, instead of a bothersome chore, I find caring for my plants enjoyable. A moment of quiet I'm so happy to have in the middle of my often packed days. Plus, gardening has been shown to decrease depression.[1]

This is a new way of living we're choosing. It's full of hope and full of possibility. We're tapping into what's already here. Happiness is already here for you. Hope is here for you. You just have to choose it.

Perhaps you'd like to use this approach as you review a list of things you have to do tomorrow or next week. Is there an item on there that you could try to begin shifting from a chore to a source of pleasure? How might you reframe walking the dog or making dinner? This practice isn't about adding anything new. It's simply about allowing what's already there to be experienced in a new, lighter way. A chance to get out in nature. An opportunity to finally try the recipe you clipped from a magazine last year.

Let's work through an example together:

- Situation: I need to water the plants.

- Thoughts: This is so much work. I'm so bad at remembering to do this. I don't think I can do it.

- Emotions: I feel overwhelmed.

- Behaviors: Avoided watering the plants. Walked past them again and again. Considered hiring somebody to help. Repeated negative thoughts. Felt even worse about myself. Plant leaves started to go brown.

- Alternate Thoughts: I'm so blessed to have these gorgeous plants that give us clean air and look so pretty in my home. I'm excited I get to water the plants today! I know this will make me feel good because I get to practice a mindfulness-based Positive Psychology intervention and check something off my Tiny Tools list. YAY!

Here's another example:

- Situation: My friends canceled dinner last minute. Now I'm on my own at home with no plans.

- Thoughts: I'm an idiot. I feel embarrassed that I was rejected like that. Even my friends don't want to spend time with me. I'm worthless.

- Emotions: I feel sad. I feel hurt.

- Behaviors: Downward spiral of negative thoughts and emotions. Cried a lot and ate junk food.

- Alternate Thoughts: I'm grateful for the extra space tonight. I get to practice self-care and I know I can make the most of this time to rest and be gentle with myself. I can look forward to seeing my friends when we reschedule.

Using this reframing approach, I was able to shift how I view folding laundry as well. To me, folding and putting away clean clothes felt like it was going to take forever, and it was a task I often left undone. Or outsourced to someone else so that I could devote myself to work where I could deliver more of an impact.

I decided to try something new. I committed to not rushing. To allowing this activity to take up the space it needed to take. Folding became a mindful exercise. In a world where we're constantly preoccupied, our minds racing with a million thoughts, I let my brain stop asking questions and I let myself be present in the moment instead.

OK, cool. I'm here in my home putting away the laundry. That's it. Nothing else needs to exist at this moment. Lift, fold, fold again.

One thing. And then the next.

Mindfulness can bring us peace. And the cool thing is we get to *choose* to be mindful.

By using a mindfulness practice, ruminating on old negative memories, being too hard on yourself, and negative future projections and worries can all be stopped in their tracks. Mindfulness helps us create a different relationship with our thoughts, feelings, and emotions. Bringing yourself back into the present can help reduce and eliminate the negative, destructive thinking that slips you down the spiral.

I used to really struggle with racing thoughts before getting to sleep. I'd feel exhausted all day and be so excited to get into bed, and then BOOM – I'd think about everything that was going wrong. These thoughts would loop over and over, replaying stories and events, and then I'd be worrying about how tired I'd feel in the morning after not getting a good night's sleep. I've since learned it can be common for ADHD brains to have racing thoughts before sleep, which for me were compounded when I went through periods of high anxiety and stress.

On those nights I'd practice this ocean breath pattern:

- Lay in bed before you sleep, close your eyes, and imagine you're on your favorite beach.

- Breathe in slowly for the count of five.

- Breathe out slowly for the count of five.

- Hear the sound of your breathing as the ocean flowing in and out at the shore.

What's one thing you could get present and mindful toward today, focusing all your energy on that one positive thing?

Your Higher Power

'It seems to me that some of us value information over wonder, and noise over silence. And I feel that we need a lot more wonder and a lot more silence in our lives.'

Fred Rogers

When people ask me what's the single best thing you've ever done for your business, my answer is easy.

Kundalini. Kundalini is known as the yoga of awareness. It incorporates repetitive movements, breathing techniques, meditation, chanting, and mantras to awaken and unblock each of the seven chakras within the body, increase consciousness, and connect you to your own divine energy.

I'm in my 11th year of Kundalini yoga practice now. It's the best thing for so many aspects of my life. For my physical health and strength, my nervous system, my prosperity, my mental clarity and awareness, and my personal power. Even for my business!

It's the kind of yoga where one day, you sit in meditation holding your arms up for 30 minutes, and the next, you're crawling around the room pretending to be a wild animal. I've experienced so much peace, bliss, and growth through this practice.

Every time I notice that I'm not feeling as good as I'd like to feel, I look at my calendar and almost inevitably discover that this daily spiritual practice has fallen off. When my teacher was sick, I noticed I was feeling significantly different, too. I hadn't been to the class in person, I'd been less consistent with attending the sessions online, and I wasn't feeling the same impact. As I've noticed in my business with events and retreats, it's essential for me to get in the room in person.

All you have to do is get in the room, Niyc. All you have to do is get on your mat. I'd tell myself this when it felt like I didn't know which way was up. Get in the room. Get on a mat. *Once you get yourself there, I promise, everything will start to shift.* Kundalini is a physical practice *and* a happiness practice. It clears negative energy and the chanting activates your voice. During times when I've felt exhausted, sick, or struggling with business or life, I've always known I could show up at the Kundalini studio and find a home within myself, within community, and with Source.

In fact, the morning I found out Sara had passed away, the first thing I did was get to class. This simple act of devotion, getting on the mat, has served me well for more than a decade. Recently, I taught Kundalini to my online community for the first time. When I shared a poll on Instagram to see if my followers would be interested, I was delighted to find this call to practice together had become my most engaging post yet!

Kundalini is designed for the whole class to be taken with your eyes closed. This means nobody is looking at anyone else, and it's really relaxing. I'm on another planet most of the time. I feel present, connected, grateful, glorious, and high. I often cry. Whether it's an emotional release or tears of bliss and gratitude, I'm there for it. The energy moves through you and gives you what you need. It creates such a clear channel and promotes clear thinking.

Tej, my teacher, calls me Nicole. Funnily enough, it's what my mum would also call me if I was in trouble! One day, when the class was being streamed online for members around the world, I was the demo at the front. Tej shouted, 'Nicole! You're doing it wrong. Everyone's got their hands out to the side. You're on the camera. Everyone's following you! You've got to do it right.'

We were laughing so much. The room is always full of camaraderie and community. I'd fucked up for the world to see, and you know what? I was OK with it!

Having a laugh. A great workout. Feeling appreciated. Connected. Sometimes, if I haven't been in class in person for a while, Tej will share that she's glad I'm there and that she feels happy when she looks at the register and sees my name. That felt so good to hear. It made *me* happy knowing my presence made her happy. It made me realize we should all do that for each other more – give voice to the joy we feel for each other.

Who can you reach out to and share that you're looking forward to seeing them?

Every time I leave my Kundalini class, I feel a shift. I feel so clear and calm. The trees are extra green. The sky is extra blue. Life feels like I'm living it in high definition. This 'after' is a big contrast to the 'before,' where I'm sometimes questioning whether to go to class in person, practice online, or not bother at all. But when I roll into class – normally just in time, as the prosperity meditation is about to start – there's always a big smile on my face because I'm so happy to be there.

In 2013 when I first began practicing Kundalini yoga, I was feeling super stuck in my life. I was in counseling to work through the aftermath of being sexually assaulted, and I was seeking relief. Looking for answers. I came across some Kundalini meditations online and it literally felt as if a dark cloud lifted from over me. I knew this was a practice for me.

In 2015 when I was planning my move to Los Angeles, the first thing I did was book a 40-day Kundalini yoga practice from the day I arrived. It helped me get grounded, have an anchor within my routine, and become part a community where I felt like I belonged. I've met some really amazing friends through Kundalini and shared many funny moments, including the time when a famous A-list actor fell asleep in class, snoring away while everybody else was praying to close out the class and gathering their belongings to leave.

I love that Kundalini is intentional, and it's a good all-in-one practice. Sometimes I feel a new focus and sense of calm. Sometimes I feel total bliss. However I feel, it's always better than I felt before class. If you don't fancy trying a full class, you can try some of the short meditations first.

Or you may want to try a different spiritual practice altogether. Kundalini (or any kind of yoga!) isn't for everyone. The idea here is to tap into a daily spiritual practice that is meaningful to you and enhances your well-being. And if you can add movement to your practice, even better!

Reflection

- Do you remember a time when you were in a room where you felt totally clear and really good? Where was it? When was it? What brought you there? Have you been back?

- How do you like to connect with Source, God, the divine, a higher power?

- What kind of rooms do you want to get into that might help to shift the way you feel?

We forget that we're all one. We forget what makes us feel good. Choose to remember, instead. When we remember our interconnectedness and our power, we'll find more light, more peace, and more opportunity.

A Sign

Guess what appeared on the windowsill of my bedroom as I was working on this book? A praying mantis. A good omen. A symbol of courage, peace, re-birth, good luck, and spiritualism, as well as mindfulness and protection. It's often associated with female empowerment and a message from the divine.

A lot of cultures have been quite fascinated with this 'devoted' creature. It was the first time I'd seen a praying mantis, and I got to sit and be present with it for some time. Another example of noticing. There's so much beauty and wonder all around when we choose to look. Remember to choose to look today.

How to Spark a Shift

'No one belongs here more than you.'
Brené Brown

In October 2021, I signed up for an eight-week Kundalini mentorship. As part of the mentorship, which was designed to lift us to higher levels of spiritual mastery, we all received a one-on-one counseling session with Tej. I felt like my biggest opportunity to create an impact was to use the session to discuss what the teachings say about suicide.

As well as sharing from the teachings, Tej also shared a personal story with me about her childhood. Tej had grown in a wealthy but abusive family where she felt she didn't belong. As a teenager, she'd been planning her own death, and it was only when a friend called her up and encouraged her to go to a yoga ashram with her that she found the desire to live.

That friend who cared enough about Tej to motivate her to start to practice yoga meant that she found a community where she grew to feel she belonged. The yoga practice and the community acted as a gateway for more positive mental health and well-being.

Tej started to work on herself and walk a spiritual path, and she's done so ever since.

There are many things we can learn from this story of recovery, which was sparked by a simple phone call from a caring friend. We can see that from the depths of struggle and despair, profound life purpose and impact can be birthed. We can learn how much power a tiny thing can have. This entire journey started from a simple step – a relationship with one person, which evolved into a daily yoga practice, which evolved into a life devoted to service. It's yet another example of what's possible when you put a Tiny Tool into action.

That's not to say you have to devote your life to service. The invitation is to just take one step... and allow the next step to appear.

A Spiritual Battle

I also want to share Tej's perspective on suicidal thoughts and behaviors. She observed that people find unity in negativity, almost like they find a sense of belonging through complaining, gossiping, and negative thinking. Negativity becomes the mantra, and the looping inside one's consciousness ushers in a downward spiral that gets stronger and stronger.

Tej spoke about how we're always either spreading the dark force or the light force through our thinking and speaking. She sees us engaged in a spiritual battle – if we're not working to stay elevated in our psyche and subconscious, the darkness can take us down.

So, what can we take from these lessons? We need to watch our own consciousness and protect it. We do that through daily spiritual practice, Positive Psychology tools, and connection with each other and with a higher power.

I believe it's super important to commit to rituals and sacred practices. It doesn't have to be complicated. We can develop some micro disciplines to do simple things that make a difference. One idea could be to reach for your phone to put on a guided meditation. It's not listening to the meditation that needs to become the habit, it's the simple act of reaching for your phone and having a go-to meditation saved for easy access. Little rituals can shift your consciousness and help you connect with yourself and your higher power. Simple rituals might include:

- splashing cold water on your face

- visiting a special, quiet place

- listening to ceremony music

- praying

- meditating

- creating a meditation corner in your home

- building an altar

- pausing and breathing in the silence

Cold Depression Kundalini Meditation

This meditation on the breath is used for healing and to break depression.

Basic position

Sit in any relaxed position with a straight spine. Relax your hands in your lap, with your palms facing up, and the left palm beneath the right. Or put your hands in *giaan mudra* (index finger curled under the thumb).

Eyes

Close your eyes nine parts of the way, leaving them just slightly open. Focus your eyes on the tip of your nose.

Breath

Inhale through the nose in four equal parts until your lungs are completely full. Exhale through the nose in one part. Four parts in, one part out.

Each part is a quick, sniff-like inhale that causes the sides of the nose to collapse in very slightly. It's important to focus on the flow of the breath, and to keep the broken breath equally divided.

Mantra

The following mantra can be mentally recited on the inhale:

Sa Ta Na Ma

On the exhale, mentally recite:

Wahe Guru

Time

Practice this for 11 minutes a day, for 40 days.

While we're in this spiritual realm, I want to offer another perspective on periods of darkness. This one comes from my friend Dr. Erin. Just before Christmas, we were out on a walk together, talking about our big visions and the work we're both here to do in the world. Erin is a Doctor of Divinity and a celebrity spiritual coach in Hollywood, helping people transform their trauma so they can live their truth.

Erin told me a story about her friend Trevor who lost his brother to addiction and went through a string of traumatic experiences which resulted in him wanting to take his own life. But he didn't.

Instead, he thought about what his father, best friend, and son, who had all passed away, would say to him in that moment. He knew they would say, 'You can't take your life.'

While Trevor had been touched by suicidal thinking, he came back from the brink with a new energy, and a clear understanding of his true mission and purpose. Trevor had already done so much spiritual and personal development work that he had the tools and inner resources to be able to deal with his own thinking and feelings in the face of his grief. In his words, he '…had to treat [his] suicidal thoughts like recovery – one day at a time.'

Erin told me this story to offer a new way of understanding these desperate moments in our lives. She reframes the times of struggle and challenge, including those times we've been right at the edge and come back from it, as a spiritual blessing, because it cracks us open to new depths and allows us to choose more alignment in our lives, where we know the true power of spiritual and personal development work to help ourselves and each other.

The greatest leaders on our planet are often those who have experienced the most darkness. Perhaps it's true that they went to the edge and came back stronger than ever and better able to move forward on the goals that mattered the most. Of course, we'd prefer never to have to get to that edge in the first place, but I like the idea of making space for this interpretation of dark periods as a time of spiritual transformation. I've been through many myself, and I believe they've forged me into a woman able to lead others into the light.

Healing through Devotion

I love the energy in the word 'devotion.' I'm devoted to the cause of preventing suicide. I'm devoted to living. While I hope to make an impact on others, it's also a commitment to myself and my soul. Devotion to myself. Devotion to the path. Something that's in service of others can be the very thing that lifts and lights you up as well. You feel supported by the universe when you call on the energy of devotion. Devotion to a mission can be devotion to ourselves.

I can't worry too much about all the big and little problems staring me in the face when I know I have work to do in the world. I *can* use Positive Psychology to help alleviate suffering. It's what I'm here to do. In the process, my soul is growing every day, finding more alignment. What a gift, right?

What do you want to devote yourself to? Where do you find meaning? Where can you find a path forward for your own soul's healing and growth? It's a beautiful place to be, once you find it. You'll still have many obstacles and decisions to make, but it's an amazing place from which to make decisions.

Let's start small – what do you want to do when you put down this book? By reading this, you've already devoted yourself to your positive mental health journey. What would be another positive decision you can make for your soul's alignment and growth?

The energy of discipline may work well for many people. *Stop making excuses; get it done.* I think there's value in that. Sometimes giving yourself a kick in the ass is a pattern interrupt you need. Other times you might need a softer approach. Ask yourself: What essence do I want to tap into today? Some days, you might be channeling the US Navy SEALs; others, you might be channeling the gentle practice of my gardener friend who waters plants as meditation. I'm not opposed to the kick-in-the-ass way of getting motivated every now and again, but sometimes life feels like it's kicking your ass enough already. Self-compassion is important as well. Slowing down. Playfulness. Ease. What if things don't need to feel so hard?

A lot of this is about tuning in to what you feel you need today. What you feel in your body. What is most supportive. Practice coming to know what feels right for you. What could help you discern which energy – discipline or devotion – is best for you? Perhaps your devotional practice becomes the simple daily ritual of taking one step each day. Devoted to yourself, your higher power, and your purpose, you keep stepping forward. You keep going for one more day.

Let's also think about your potential role as a gatekeeper to help someone else who is suffering. Throughout this book, we've been talking about how you can create change by devoting yourself to your own healing. Looking after yourself first. Filling up your own cup instead of trying to pour from an empty one.

When we have access to a psychological toolkit, we're able to center ourselves when we feel dysregulated. We're able to cope better and reach for healthy mechanisms to help us. We can go out into the world feeling more energized, capable, and grateful. It feels that little bit easier to show up, give support, share a smile, or help somebody else. We're able to forgive more easily, reframe our thoughts more quickly, and hold on to hope more powerfully.

Imagine you've already checked some items off your Tiny Tools list by 10 a.m. You've allowed heavy feelings to move through your body and get released? You've laughed, sang, danced, and chanted instead of scrolling on social media? You've opened up and had a fulfilling conversation with a supportive friend over a cup of tea? Having done these things, you might be able to support someone else more easily, too. Your raised awareness might mean that you're able to smile at the delivery person. Offer a helping hand to an elderly lady packing groceries into her car. Forgive yourself for a simple but time-consuming mistake. Recognize your strengths and put them to use. Appreciate the sight of the moon.

The ripple effect of Positive Psychology is activated more easily when you resource yourself first.

In my coaching practice, we teach our frameworks using a three-step process – learn, embody, integrate. The same applies here. You discover the tools from Positive Psychology. You apply them for yourself first and experience the positive shifts. Then you integrate them into your own life and take them out into the world to help others. That middle step about taking the tools and doing the work for yourself, so you feel strong and resourced. If you miss that step, you'll feel uncertain and wobbly. If we all follow the process, when we go out into the world we'll have the tools and the energy to listen, support, and help others move toward their goals. Resourcing yourself makes it possible for you to better support others.

Like many of us, I used to wear being overtired like a badge of honor. I'm so busy! I'm running, running, running. I only got four hours of sleep! No more.

I learned how important it is to rest and get good quality sleep to heal, both physically and mentally. Physically, I needed deep rest to heal from the mold poisoning I told you about earlier. I also found that as I was emotionally healing from other big life events I needed extra rest; it was like my mind was protecting itself to deal with traumatic experiences and the aftershock.

The following choices helped me:

- I chose to simplify and focus on a 'sleep-first' mental health and well-being plan. I knew if I was well rested, I'd have a better chance of feeling better.

- I chose to turn my bedroom into a healing sanctuary.

- I chose to switch my phone off by 9 p.m. each night.

- I chose to be in bed between 9 and 10:30 p.m. and asleep by 11 p.m.

- I chose to take a natural magnesium-based supplement to support relaxation and quality sleep.

- I chose to install a white noise machine in my bedroom.

- I chose to wake up without an alarm.

- I chose to install a meditation cushion in the corner of my bedroom so I could practice my Tiny Tools more easily.

I use the words 'choices' and 'chose' intentionally because remember – you can choose. Tiny steps.

Good sleep is a pillar of mental health – health in general, actually. The four pillars of health are sleep, nutrition, movement, and restoration.[1] Being overtired depletes your willpower, meaning your decision-making is impacted. If I don't get enough sleep, I have less mental clarity, make poor decisions, and I'm more likely to start feeling burnout. It's a vicious cycle. You can change your thinking patterns and raise your awareness through better sleep. It's a simple place to start.

By getting enough rest, you can further devote yourself and your energy to your own positive mental health journey, and the things that matter the most to you. You'll shore yourself up to be steady for someone else.

With enough healing (and sleep!), we'll grow in this practice of devotion together, linking arms around the world as a solid force. What we've got at the moment are isolated and fragmented methodologies and interventions for dealing with mental health and preventing suicide. What I'm envisioning is something where we're more connected and really present for each other. This is what I mean by the new tapestry we're weaving. The new story. A world without suicide.

Overwhelm

As I write this morning, I'm in comfy clothes and I've got my hair tied up. I have one online meeting coming up, but I'll use audio only and won't turn on the camera. I just had a great session lying on my infrared mat. So, I'm kind of in this calm vibe. I take a breath. I'm here. I've got it under control. Then my phone buzzes. It's a message from my colleague Anna: *That promotion you want to do, Niyc? We need eight selfie photos in four different outfits.*

And... I'm off.

I do my makeup. Hair. Assemble the lights. Choose outfits. Take new photos. Write copy. Answer questions. Come up with new ideas. Quick! Go, go, go. On calls. Off calls. I have to get this done.

Some days my feet don't touch the ground. Other days feel spacious AF. I love the variety of both. And yes, I have to be micromanaged to get photos done (thanks Anna, you're making my gratitude list today!)

We're so conditioned to fill our days, to be productive. Hyper-productive. It's exhausting sometimes.

It's also kind of fascinating, isn't it? This society we've built. It's almost like you live with a chronic low level of anxiety, where your body and your nervous system can't rest because you're continually thinking about, generating, and consuming content, with no time to process or integrate your experiences. Except your nervous system *can* rest if you get intentional about it. If I don't have space and time to think, then I feel overwhelmed. Sure, I can keep going like a Duracell bunny for a sprint. But none of us are designed to be 'on' all of the time. Remember, you'll approach everything from a better place when you've had a good night's sleep.

We have to focus on our well-being. We have to be intentional and create routines with well-being at the center. Take a step back. Start to consider what you need. Build your healing sanctuary in your home. Walk. A cup of tea. A chat with a neighbor. Time in nature. So many of the items on the Tiny Tools list counteract the complex demands and over-stimulation of our lives. I know the tools as a Positive Psychologist, yet I can still get caught up in the next demand and the next and the next. I have to remind myself to pause. Be gentle. Go slow.

We're not going to try the tools once or twice and become entirely new people. Instead, we have to commit to using the tools many times and creating a new way to be.

It's also important to understand the power of creating space for ourselves. For a while, I was rolling into my therapy sessions feeling frantic about how much stuff I had to do. I'd be almost unable to start the conversation, letting out a huge sigh as I joined the call. Over time, I started to appreciate how that appointment gave me space. A container for creative conversations, ideas, and inspirations. A place to offload energy and work through emotions. Taking that time was essential. It gave me a moment to step back from the overwhelming list of 'must-do' things, tugging at me from all angles, and ask myself: *What do I really need to do today?*

Yes, I do want and need to support my students. And I do need to keep writing this book. And I do need to keep taking steps. But I think we need to reframe our 'must-dos' or, maybe more accurately, we need to *expand* them to include activities that promote and support our well-being. Without that, the businesses, the book, the obligations to others, all of it will just fall apart anyway. So, your priority list can't be just business and keeping the house running and taking care of the kids. It also has to include taking care of yourself.

Reflection

- What do you need in your day?

- What helps you feel supported?

- What helps you feel filled up?

- What do you need to feel healthy and optimized?

- How might you create space in your day today?

Take time to think about these questions. Perhaps over the course of the following week, you can make it a point to notice what you need. Take notes. Think it over. Bring it to a conversation with a trusted friend, therapist, coach, or relative.

- When do the days seem to be working?

- What is it about a particular day that felt good?

- What brings you back when you're thrown off course?

With this practice, you'll start to develop your own Tiny Tools list, full of activities that work best for you.

Get Out, Self-Doubt

During a ceremonial girls' night, my friends Anna and Sahara told me that I'm always so playful and light even when I'm navigating tough stuff. I received the compliment gratefully, and at the same time thought *WTAF*? Here I was battling nihilism, thinking I'm cynical AF, and feeling like I'm doing a terrible job of everything. Perspective is a wonderful thing! Hearing that my friends see this in me gave me such a boost and I felt lighter navigating everything from then on.

Being on a mission to help the world become more positive and mentally healthy, and having been on my own journey of mental health too, has definitely offered me a vast perspective.

Well-being can fluctuate, based on what you're experiencing in life. The key is how you respond. It's all in the response. It's in the pause. The breath. The assessment. The reflection, and the *intentional* next step. At different stages of your journey, your needs will change. It's important to reflect on what is and what isn't working for you. What new interventions do you need to try? What could you do differently? More of? Less of?

Once again, it's being intentional about how you proceed. Not just accepting something because that's how you've always done it or because it's the first way you think of. What got you here isn't what's going to get you to your next phase of growth.

It doesn't have to be perfect. You do have to start.

Here's what I'm doing at the moment: I'm journaling, keeping my body moving, taking care of my sleep, and making sure I don't have too many commitments on my calendar. Even though seeing friends makes me feel good, seeing too many things in my calendar can feel overwhelming. If I've got too much going on, I sometimes get a feeling of dread that I might feel worn out by my days. I suspect this is true for many of us. It's a lesson that we can continue to intentionally practice, based on how we feel.

Positive Psychology can't make your life perfect all the time. But it can make it better *more* of the time. Positive Psychology gives a higher sense of agency and capability to make changes and shift mood. It allows you to hold on to hope, stay devoted, and stay connected. Those are the lifelines.

I will say that without the tools that I'm sharing with you in this book, I wouldn't know how to move forward on my darker days. I might have given up. It's a sobering thought. Without finding Positive Psychology all those decades ago, I might not be here. Tools for hope. That's the difference here – I have the resources to alleviate the struggle. I always have a pathway out, a way to find relief.

One of the interventions I came back to over the weekend was writing myself a forgiveness letter. When someone's being too hard on themselves, this letter can offer relief and release.

I took out my journal and I wrote out the sentence: *I owe myself an apology.* Then I started writing all the things I wanted to apologize to myself for having done.

Self-abandonment came up. It's a theme that's come up for me a lot over the years, but it felt especially poignant in this instance.

I forgive myself for making misaligned choices.

I forgive myself for being too hard on myself.

I forgive myself for all of the times I didn't listen to my intuition.

Does this ever happen to you? Are there moments where you get a flash of intuition? Where something feels off? Do you choose to honor it or ignore it?

I forgive myself for abandoning my alignment.

I forgive myself for abandoning my boundaries.

All things I value so deeply. It's not like I'd simply abandoned my commitment to cut back on desserts. This was a deep internal reckoning. Radical self-honesty will create breakthroughs. I owed myself quite a profound apology.

Here's what I also did. I took responsibility for the reality I'd chosen. The forgiveness letter turned into a gratitude letter. I forgave myself for not nourishing and nurturing myself. But I also acknowledged that I'm grateful for how I've shown up with compassion and how I've always, *always,* done my best through whatever life has thrown at me.

I feel proud to say that so purely. I've always done my best. It reminds me of a phrase from Kundalini: *'Do your best, and let God do the rest.'*

I've always tried to make the most loving choices I can.

I've done my best to hold compassion in my heart and to protect my energy and my well-being.

I know how to center myself so I can move through the world with more gentle power, ease, and grace. When I make a move now, it's from an empowered place.

It's my spiritual grounding that allows me to show up with grace, no matter what the challenge. I like to keep the broader spiritual context in my mind and the idea that we're all one in my heart. What we do to another person, we're also doing to ourselves because the whole universe is interconnected.

Everything Is Serving Your Growth

What if we tried to look at our lives with the idea that everything is serving our growth? We don't have to believe it's true. Instead, let's experiment. We're going to approach everything today with the understanding that all we encounter is serving our growth.

With this approach, it's always possible to find the gold within, even in the most challenging situations. Even in the hard stuff, there's always so much beauty to be found, if we know to look for it. This entire book is, I hope, an offering of peace and a gentle path forward that came out of grief. It can feel like everything is terrible, the worst you've ever felt, but when you pause and take the time to reflect, you can always find something that's offering guidance and growth.

It may take a long time to see it. Sometimes years or even decades. But stay on the path of discovery and look for that guidance. On the other hand, you might discover it in an instant, without having to wait a long time. You might find it right now!

Find the Gold Within

Think of a difficult experience you've had recently. Ask yourself:

- What was it that felt hard?

- What was it that was challenging?

- How has that situation served you?

Sometimes it's so hard to find the gold within when it feels like you're running a mental health marathon, and something's got to give. I struggle with that, too. I feel frustrated at times. 'There's a lesson in this, Niyc!' I tell myself, but inside, I feel like I can't get out of the negative loop. I don't know what to do next. I feel like I can't catch a break. Are there really *always* blessings and lessons? Can we always look for the silver lining? Is it always the right thing to do?

In my experience, it's beneficial to look for the lessons on both a micro and a macro scale. What can you garner from a very specific element of a challenging experience? Let's say somebody is hurrying through their morning and accidentally bumps their car on a curb. The micro lesson might be not to rush, and to practice mindfulness moving through the morning. Then if you zoom out and look more broadly, there might be a bigger perspective or lesson to learn. What if this same person had been feeling anxious and activated in their nervous system because of a relationship they were in, in which they felt they always had to walk on eggshells? The broader lesson might be learning to listen better to the intuitive nudges that suggest it was the wrong relationship in the first place.

And the blessings? They might be thankful nobody was hurt in the accident. Or grateful they received these insights so they can make a positive change.

It's important not to feign positivity, to bypass the experience itself or the feeling associated with it. You don't have to put a brave face on it. You can acknowledge that things feel shit right now. And know you're on the path. Taking steps. Using the tools. Harnessing hope. Practicing devotion. Nourishing connection. One more day.

Toxic Positivity

I want to take a moment to talk about toxic positivity. This kind of false buoyancy happens when we pretend everything is fine! When we don't acknowledge pain. When we don't allow ourselves or our loved ones to sit with what is present. When we're unwilling to pull at the roots. It's a kind of spiritual bypassing. It's being told, 'Just think positive' when that actually means suppressing and repressing real emotions that need to be moved through you.

When we immediately jump to the growth, we're not honoring how hard life can feel. When we go straight to the lesson, we're skipping a step. In other places in this book, I've talked about trying to maintain the perspective that *all is in the service of our growth*, but by 'all' I mean our pain as well.

Our confusion, our loneliness, our frustration, our heartache. We don't get to skip it and leapfrog right to the pedestal of how our soul has grown, because we might not be there yet.

It's not always honest. And it doesn't always support. We have emotions for a reason. We don't have to be happy all the time. Toxic positivity skips over the important step of embodiment (*see page 109*). Instead of jumping to 'think positive,' be present.

Let's say someone doesn't do what they say they're going to do. Intellectually, I understand that they're just busy but perhaps on that particular day, it really lands in a painful way for me. I can acknowledge that I'm not feeling so great. That it sucks. I feel sad. I can take a step back and pause to understand from a more regulated space that it's not actually about me being let down or rejected. That was the *feeling* I had. Maybe it's indicating my inner child is feeling rejected. Unloved. Toxic positivity puts on the brave face and keeps on keeping on. But that limits my capacity to process.

Instead, I can choose to notice the way the feeling is expressing itself in my body and my nervous system. I can think about what it reminds me of. Get curious. Was it anything to do with when I was a young girl who was bullied at school? How can I nurture that part of myself? And once I've processed for myself, I'll share with my friend from an empowered place. Non-combative. But not bypassing either.

Feel.

Process.

And release.

Reach for your Tiny Tools to self-soothe. If you're in public, maybe there isn't much you can do other than some deep breathing. But once you're back home, you could:

- light candles
- put on some soothing music
- journal
- take a warm bath
- wrap yourself in soft blankets
- allow yourself to cry or scream into a pillow (or both!)

Plus, know the work that you're doing daily will shift the way you feel generally, too, so these acute experiences won't bother you as much as they used to. The compound effect in action and your positive emotions are building your psychological toolkit every day.

And if you ever want to take out your rage in a controlled way in public, here in LA, they have rage rooms where you can go into a room and express your rage safely by smashing old computers. Or you could try boxing, instead!

Expression helps you offload energy and emotion to free up capacity.

Reflection

- What helps you process and release emotions in a positive way?

- What makes you feel like you have the resources to support a courageous conversation?

- How can you find time today to practice processing and releasing emotions in a safe way?

Practice on something small: a rude neighbor, an unfair (but easily handled) request from your boss, or a delayed train. Build up your resources. Pause. Strengthen your processing and self-soothing muscles. What do you need to do for yourself before you talk to the neighbor or the boss to bring yourself to a regulated state and give yourself the best chance of a productive exchange?

Eventually, instead of meeting these challenges with immediate frustration, you'll come at them from a place of abundance. Not toxic positivity, but rather life-giving possibility.

Choices.

Options.

Freedom.

Growth.

Shifting the Ratio

The 3:1 positivity ratio means that it takes three to five good thoughts or communications to outweigh one bad one. When we get stuck in thinking about all that's going wrong and being too hard on ourselves, we're energizing our suffering, and slipping into a downward spiral. Instead, we want to energize our goals and positive mental health journey. Negative thinking lowers the frequency of our energy and body in just three seconds, whereas it takes 21 seconds to shift your frequency back up. If we can decrease our negativity, as well as increase our positivity, it'll be easier to maintain a facilitative ratio balance.

We can't always control what goes wrong, but we can shift our perspective. That's the superpower we have to hold on to throughout this book. So, let me ask you: What are you doing right now to shift your perspective? If you feel yourself going down a path of negative thinking, worrying about everything you need to do, mistakes you've made, and things that aren't working out, take a pause. Are you energizing the downward spiral? Or the upward spiral? Negative thoughts and feelings energize more of the same. And the same premise holds for positive thoughts, so why not focus on those?

All the to-dos and challenges will still be there, but you can lift your mood and better empower yourself to handle them. Can you phone a supportive friend? Can you go to the store and ask the checkout person how he or she's doing? Can you do something kind for a neighbor?

Our days will always be a mix of good and bad, up and down. You have the power to shift the ratio for yourself, and someone else.

There's a famous expression, 'What you focus on grows.' Thoughts are powerful.

Ripples. Upward spirals. Our thoughts, our conversations, and our kindness ripple outward and upward and bring us together, for one more day.

It's Safe to Feel

'Crying, mourning, lamenting are all incredibly underrated in our society which, is crazy because the experience of crying can actually help us feel moments of grace. And we need that. We need grace right now more than ever.'
Chloé S. Valdary

The body plays a powerful role in mental health. Positive Psychology isn't just about the mind; we process emotions through our bodies whether we like it or not. When I feel a strong emotion – whether it's sadness or anxiety or fear – I often stop and ask myself this question: What am I feeling in my body? That helps me locate the emotion, truly feel my way through it, breathe, and begin to process it. The more I do this in the moment, the more the emotion flows and the less it gets stuck. Allowing ourselves to process through the body is so important and can create big shifts in the way we feel.

Somatic exercises emphasize the link between our mind and body. They help us get out of our heads and can shift our attention and focus from overthinking or ruminating toward whatever practice we're doing.

My Pilates trainer Reiko is excellent at helping me relax my mind during our workouts. If I arrive at our session from a busy working day, she gives me complicated exercises that shut me up and require me to focus on only the exercise. Afterward, I feel so peaceful and realize I haven't thought about any of the things I had on my mind beforehand.

Somatic exercise doesn't mean you have to go to the gym – there are lots you can practice quickly, simply, and easily from the comfort of your bedroom.

Our bodies store emotions and memories without us even realizing it, and every time you experience something acutely stressful, you give that thing a meaning, and file the memory away in your brain.

The jaw and the hip flexors are common areas for emotions to be stored. You might notice when you start to tune in to your body more that you can really feel the release of tension in these areas when you massage and stretch them out. You may feel emotions come up, and you might even cry.

Simple Somatic Exercises

Pause right now and try these simple somatic exercises:

- Relax your jaw. Open your mouth wide. Breathe. Massage your jaw muscles. Touch the roof of your mouth with your tongue. Breathe. Stick your tongue out.

- Practice eye yoga: Look to one side and then the other. Look down. Then look up.

- Roll your shoulders up, back, and down. Breathe deeply. As you exhale, allow a sigh or any other sound to be released.

- Stretch your arms upward. Inhale. Sweep your arms downward and exhale.

- Take three long, deep breaths. Place one hand on your heart and the other on your rib cage. Feel the connection to your body.

Notice how you feel after practicing this simple routine – I just practiced it too while writing this and feel instantly better. Lighter. More calm. Less tense.

The fact is your body is an amazing tool which is programmed to protect you. So, if your brain categorizes an experience as traumatic or hard, your nervous system exhibits a fight, flight, freeze, or fawn response to keep you safe from the perceived danger. The body then files the memory away so you can get on with day-to-day life. But it's still there. And it still needs to be processed.

I remember being trapped in a bathroom, looking into the vacant, black eyes of my then-boyfriend, feeling terrified and fearing for my life. He'd struck me on the head and then followed me into the bathroom when I'd tried to get away. Now he was blocking the door, grabbing both of my wrists, and kicking me in the ankle at the same time, goading me to call the police.

My nervous system was in overdrive, and I was physically shaking, wondering if this was how I was going to die. I stayed calm, didn't raise my voice, and tried to think fast about how I was going to stay alive. After more than four hours of saying I was exhausted and wanted to sleep, I managed to get out of the bathroom and collapse into bed, silently sobbing and hoping it wouldn't start all over again.

After that my body went into a functional freeze state. I could still operate to the extent I was keeping everything looking normal and stable on the surface, but there was more to the story – and my body was keeping the score behind the scenes. I felt numb, like I was just going through the motions. I'd enjoy spending time with friends less and felt disconnected from myself and the world around me. I also started to notice I'd been holding my breath a lot. Knowing what I know from my work, I reached for tools to help myself.

I accepted a referral to a trauma crisis center, which felt unnecessary at the time – I was putting on a good act of pretending everything was fine, after all. I practiced somatic exercises, sat in ceremony with plant medicines like ayahuasca, committed to harnessing hope, doubled down on devotion, allowed friends to support me, and – most importantly – I got to safety and got out of that relationship. Taking positive action, even when I felt uncomfortable doing so, saved my life.

Shamanic shaking is one of my favorite somatic exercises and I practice it daily. I've always loved shaking around during Kundalini and have a super special memory with my friend Briana where she led me in this practice after ceremony. We shook and danced and let out so many sighs and sounds in nature as we moved energy through our bodies and let all that shit go!

Shamanic Shaking Exercise

This practice is really simple:

- Stand up and plant your feet firmly on the floor. Barefoot on the earth – even better.

- Start to bounce in place and shake your hands. Shake your wrists, your arms. Shake your booty, shake your entire body!

- Stomp on the floor (and if the neighbors complain, feel free to blame me!).

- Let out a sigh. Stretch your jaw. Let out a roar.

- If there's a specific event or tension you've experienced within your day, put your focus on that as you shake. Notice where you feel the energy and emotion in your body and allow it to be shaken out and released.

- Whatever wants to come through and come out of you, allow it. Bless it and release it.

I practice this for the length of one song. Usually something jungly with a big beat. Then my playlist shifts to a slower song to flow and dance to. You can shift your shake into gentle grace and movement, ending in gratitude and thanks.

A Rush of Light

One message I want to be sure makes its way through this book is that we always have hope. Hold on to that, hard. Maybe as you're reading these words right now, you're having a tough day. I need you to know that there will be a better day. I know this. I've lived through those dark days, too. The days when escape feels like the only option. But a tiny bit of hope can keep us here today, and then one more day after that. Even if it's just the faintest flicker. A glimmer. A crack of light at the end of the tunnel. That trust, that faith, will get you through.

Choose to hold on to that hope. It's a choice you get to make. The broader suicidology research tells us that hopelessness is generally understood as a major risk factor for suicide, and fatal suicide attempts happen not because the person wants to die but rather because they give up hope for living. Through my research for *One More Day*, I discovered from conversations with first responders that there's almost always evidence of the person changing their mind at the last minute, and desperately trying to live. Therefore, it's critical that we find ways to harness the energy of hope.

Sometimes hope can feel far away. Abstract, as if it isn't real. I've had more than a few nihilistic moments when I've thought, *What's the point, anyway?* In those moments, you have to fight. You have the Tiny Tools to help you. Remember to reach for one of them. Choose the one that feels the easiest for you. And then reach for another. You've already reached for this book – that's a step in the right direction. You opened it up. You're reading these words. Reading a section of this book might be a Tiny Tool for you in itself!

You don't have to know how you'll feel after you try a Tiny Tool, but there's a good chance that you'll feel at least a *tiny* bit better. A tiny bit stronger. That's what we're going for here. Not life-changing miracles, but small shifts. Little possibilities. Which really can turn out to be life-saving miracles. When you reach for a tool, practice an exercise or intervention, get outside, experience a positive shift, a little chink of light finds its way through the clouds. A little more hope is allowed in. Hope. Devotion. Connection.

What drives me in writing this book is the genuine energy of knowing Positive Psychology can help. After Sophie passed away, I didn't know whether to write about it. Eventually I got to a place where I knew I couldn't *not* write about it, because the call to service was so strong. We still have so much work to do to get the science of suicide prevention into people's daily lives so they can practice and benefit from the shifts in well-being it affords. And the good news is, there's more evidence and research available every day to guide us in making these changes in powerful ways.

Pause and meditate on the following phrases:

Powerless to powerful.

Hopelessness to hopefulness.

I can always take one small step.

One Small Step

Feelings of helplessness often accompany suicidal ideation, and those feelings can be fleeting. So, it's super powerful to know that we're never completely helpless, that we can always take one small step. With this small exercise comes the reclamation of your power:

- Right now, take three deep breaths.

- Breathe in, call your power back.

- Breathe out, say 'thank you.'

- Breathe in, call your power back.

- Breathe out, say 'yes' to hope.

- Breathe in, call your power back.

- Breathe out, congratulate yourself.

You just took a small step.

My story

This book is for people who are struggling to hold on for one more day as well as those who are by their side. I've been both. I've lived what I'm writing. I've felt this and I continue to feel it every now and again. That's where this book comes from. It comes from a really deep place. A deeply personal place. Yes, Positive Psychology is my life's work. But suicide prevention – this mission grew out of some of the darkest moments of my own life.

My first and only attempt at taking my own life happened when I was 11 years old, while I was being badly bullied during my first year at high school. After being surrounded by a ring of kids at lunchtime with another girl who wanted a fight, I started to feel terrified to go to school. I can still hear the exact words and sounds of the kids shouting and encouraging the fight. Growing up, I remember you found yourself in one of two camps: You'd either been taught that if someone hits you, you walk the other way, or if someone hits you, you hit them back twice as hard. I was part of the former schooling, whereas my opponent was the latter.

I felt OK during scheduled lesson times when there was structure and the teacher could keep an eye on things. But as soon as the school bell rang and we headed out of class to catch the bus home, it would start. Tuesdays were particularly bad because we had a Physical Education lesson, and there was no structure in the class. I'd dread getting dressed in the changing rooms and going into the sports hall. I'd move slowly and keep my head down. I occasionally tried pretending I was sick to get out of class, but that never seemed to work. Moving through life feeling scared every second was tough, and I was only 11 years old. It seems like another lifetime and another person entirely, recalling this to you now. And at the same time, it feels like it all happened yesterday.

One Tuesday morning before heading out to school, I felt like I couldn't face the bullying anymore. I just wanted it to be over. I raided my mum's medicine cabinet and took her pills. When I started to feel unwell, I told my mum what I'd done. She burst into tears, phoned my dad, and asked him to leave work and meet us at the hospital. After that, I was home-schooled for six months while my parents tried to get me a place in a new school in the middle of the year.

I felt so much shame for what I'd done. For what I'd put my parents through. And I didn't want anybody to know. But people were asking questions about why I'd disappeared from class. My mum encouraged me to share with some of my long-standing friends, who I'd known since primary school, about what I'd done. They were so amazing and supportive, and we're still in touch today. The grace, care, love, and loyalty they showed me way back then really helped me rebuild my confidence and myself. Even as a kid I was able to experience the power of social support, a sense of belonging, and positive relationships with these friends – even if I was too young to understand that's what it was at the time.

After months of trying to get into another school with no success, my parents decided to re-mortgage our family home so they could afford to pay for me to go to private school. My friend Jenny, who lived down the street, went to the same school, and I'd always heard great things about it. It was my opportunity to start a new life.

Since then, I've had suicidal thoughts on a handful of other occasions, including when I was really sick and struggling to sleep, when I was taking steps to get out of an unsafe relationship, and I was doing the healing work after being sexually assaulted. But I did the work; I flattened the emotion around the story. It's been neutralized as an event that happened which now doesn't bring up any emotion within me. I have my friend Dr. Erin to thank for this, and the counselors at the Rape Crisis center back in Newcastle, UK, who did an amazing job of guiding me through the portal of darkness to help me find the light.

They helped me feel hopeful. And when I think of how my story might help others – not because of what happened to me, but because of who I've gone on to become even though it did, and the strength and happiness and success I've been able to experience since then – it makes it non-negotiable for me to share it. I know that when I read about people who had thrived through adversity, it made me feel more hopeful that I could too, even if I didn't feel like it or know how to at the time.

I'm now going to share some further details about the sexual assault that happened to me, so if you find this content distressing or triggering, please do skip ahead to the next section.

When I was 25, during the last stretch of my master's program, I went on vacation to Spain with some girlfriends. We met two friendly guys at a beach club one afternoon and went for a big group lunch with them two days later, just before I had to catch my flight back to Amsterdam, where I was living at the time. When the lunch was over, I said goodbye and planned to hop on a bus to the airport, but one of the men was adamant that he'd call his driver to take me. This wasn't unusual – we all used drivers to and from the airport, after all. So I thought nothing of it, and thanked him.

When the car arrived, one of the men got into the back with me and the driver began the journey to the airport. As soon as the car set off, the demeanor of the man changed, and I knew I was in trouble. Knowing I had no way of escape in a moving car and in unfamiliar territory, the man then sexually assaulted me. I remember hearing the unusual foreign music, and seeing the green of the mountains and blue of the sky flying past the windows as we made the twists and turns through the hills. The driver ignored my screams and desperate attempts to push my attacker off me. Instead, he turned up the music, then reached backward between the seats and grabbed one of my legs to stop me from kicking and fighting back.

When it was over, I assumed the men would ditch me at the side of the road, but they dropped me off at the airport, bags and all, as if nothing had happened. I ran into the terminal and landed in the arms of a stranger, who hugged me and said she'd seen us a few days earlier at the beach club. She worked there and said to me, 'He's a bad man, a criminal, a bad man.' She asked if she could take me to the airport hospital but I knew I was about to miss my flight, so I thanked her and sprinted for my gate.

For two whole years, I couldn't talk about it. I blocked it out as if it never happened. I went through all kinds of unhealthy coping mechanisms. Then I started having flashbacks, and my world came crashing down. Finally, I told my parents, forced myself to start going to counseling (even though I never felt like I had anything to say), and tiny step by tiny step, I began to heal.

Moving forward

With every traumatic thing I've experienced, I've eventually been able to crawl forward slowly enough to rebuild. To bounce back. To create a new and more aligned version of myself. It's never been a case of waving a magic wand. It's been an unglamorous step-by-step process of accepting reality, opening my heart to friends, leaning into therapy, trusting in a higher power, and trusting in myself. Each time I've embraced this pathway of hope, no matter how small and dull that chink of light at the time, I've found myself more empowered, *through* the pain.

Writing about these subjects could theoretically bring me back to a state of grief – but instead, I have feelings of joy, hope, and light. I'm stronger and happier now than I've ever been. Through my exploration of my growth, I've learned about how others can explore themselves too, and become more psychologically, emotionally, spiritually, and physically resourced so they can navigate tough times and come to deeply enjoy all that life has to offer. When we're intentional about our journey of personal development we can learn, grow, and thrive. Moving through so many extremely challenging experiences in my own life has given me a depth of feeling and understanding which both compels my mission and allows me to hold a more powerful space for others through my work.

My friend Kyle taught at one of my retreats in 2022. Kyle is a spiritual teacher and angel expert. (Pretty cool, right?) On the last morning, we had breakfast together overlooking the ocean, and we were chatting about the concept of this book. When I shared about Sophie and our pact, Kyle said he literally got chills all over his body. 'You have angelic support here,' Kyle told me. He said he felt a big rush of light coming through when I spoke about *One More Day*. I got chills too – and I knew the pact was still on. Even though I hadn't been able to save Sophie, I had work to do to prevent more people from taking their own lives.

A rush of light.

How beautiful is that? The opposite of the darkness. We can talk about one of the toughest topics in the world – the desire someone has to end their life – and these conversations can be accompanied by a rush of light. Maybe they can *be* a rush of light. A rush of light that helps you remember you're supported. When you harness hope, remember how much you matter, and know that you belong here with the rest of us right alongside you, perhaps you'll feel that rush of light, too.

Meaning

I've told you quite a bit about my life's purpose. This book is a testament to it. It's taken me years of lessons, career changes, relationship changes, multiple moves across the ocean, navigating depression, and a ton of introspection, but I now have a pretty good sense of who I am and what I want to make of my life.

Understanding who you are and what's important to you can make your life more meaningful. This process is proven to help you flourish in life and is shown to be a good protective factor against suicide. Even if someone doesn't have meaning yet, actively searching for it will still positively impact their well-being and willingness to live. Finding meaning, in essence, helps give people more reasons to live.

Survivor Story

What helped you get through one more day?

Reminding myself how important it was that my son continued to have a mother and that this wasn't about me - I [had] to think about those left behind. Realizing [how much] it would impact them and color their lives forever was what brought me away from the thoughts. I'd hate for them to suffer on my account. Also, I know through life experience that things don't stay the same for very long, so I just told myself to hold on for a day, a week, the next few weeks, and tried to find things to be hopeful about to pull myself out of the despair. Crying helped, too. Being sad that I had got to that point when I knew I had so much to offer the world.

Survivor

Meaningful Photography

Reflecting on memories can help you connect with a deeper sense of meaning within.

– Take a moment to think about a memory which brings up positive emotions for you, or one that feels particularly meaningful.

– Find a photograph of the memory, or take a photograph of something that symbolizes the meaningful memory, that you can look at again in the future.

– Start a digital folder on your phone or print out your photos and add to your Hope Box (*see page 38*).

Some of my favorite meaningful photos are of my first graduation ceremony, cuddles with my niece and nephew, and moments captured in nature.

When Did You Stop?

'In many shamanic societies, if you came to a medicine person complaining of being disheartened, dispirited, or depressed, they would ask one of four questions. When did you stop dancing? When did you stop singing? When did you stop being enchanted by stories? When did you stop finding comfort in the sweet territory of silence?'
Gabrielle Roth

When my student Iona shared the quote above on social media, I really felt it. It reminded me of the strength of our spirit and the simplicity in nurturing our soul. If I look at the tools and practices that work for me to move emotions and energy through my body, I notice that I love to move, I love to shake, I love to chant, I love to sing. I love the feeling of fascination I get when I ask questions and the awe I feel when discovering more about somebody else. I'm grateful every day to have peace in my heart and peace in my home. Living through years of having neither makes the depth of feeling thankful more profound than ever.

This is yet another reminder that some of the simplest things can be the most powerful for our well-being. But only when we remember them. When I was struggling the most, I found it really difficult to remember to do the most basic of things, never mind try to muster up the energy to dance. But when I did? I felt infinitely better.

Of course, positive emotions alone don't cure depression, but they can go some way toward building resources to prevent people from becoming vulnerable and alleviating the pressure in those who are depressed. The experience of more negative emotions and a lack of positive emotions is highly correlated with suicidal ideation. You can live with more hopefulness and productivity when you focus on experiencing more positive emotions first.

Was there a time when instead of scrolling through social media, you'd play your favorite album and dance around the room? Was there a time when silence felt sacred and peaceful, rather than stifling and unbearable? Was there a time when you'd call your friend and laugh together for hours, rather than texting to avoid talking on the phone?

When did you stop?

What used to give you a lift? What used to make you laugh? Maybe you need to add some of that back into your life. With this tapestry we're weaving, it's not only about learning new interventions and exercises. Some of it means circling back to what we knew when we were kids. How to have fun. How to not take ourselves too seriously. How to sing along to a favorite song at the top of our voices.

Discover a spiritual path

The quote at the start of this chapter comes from shamanic teaching. I think singing, dancing, letting loose, and having fun can be a gateway toward a spiritual experience and that's the topic I'd like to turn to now.

I didn't really have a spiritual practice growing up. I'd go to church every now and again on a Sunday and I loved singing hymns in school – I always got chills singing about grace, blessings, and a higher wisdom. My spiritual practice really began to develop when I discovered Gregg Braden's book *Divine Matrix* as a teenager and Wayne Dyer's work, too. It was my exploration of Positive Psychology, though, which really led me along a spiritual path. I learned about the scientific benefits of practices like meditation, mindfulness, awe, gratitude, and love, and started to practice rituals within my day. Now I see all of life as ceremony and ritual. Building a spiritual practice, even something super simple in your day, can help bring you comfort, peace, structure, and hope.

Given all the divisiveness and fear in the world, it's very easy to slip into negative or even catastrophic thinking. After just a glance at the daily headlines, it's easy to see why we need to build and maintain our spiritual practice. That practice will help us clear the chaos and stay in the right mind. Maintaining hopefulness, being devoted, and staying connected will all help you on your positive healing path.

Do you want to live a life of fear or a life of liberation? A liberated life will come from within us, not from anything going on around us. A liberated life means saying 'yes' to your spiritual practice.

If I ever feel worried about something or things are really scary and hard, I devote more time to my spiritual practice. It always helps me feel stronger and clearer, regardless of what chaos is going on around me. After a Kundalini class, I find I'm able to walk with more lightness than before, and with a greater sense of personal power and a deeper feeling of presence. My teacher said to always remember your 'royalness' as you move through your day – I really feel that after I practice and walk with my shoulders back and my head held high.

The word 'devotion' comes forward here again – the idea of devotion to self and to something bigger than us. You might be concerned about how much time it will take to commit to a daily spiritual practice – after all, there are only so many hours in a day. To address this, I encourage you to think less about what you're missing during the time you dedicate to something like yoga (or whatever works for you in this space), and more about what it is you're *gaining*. The clear mind, the centered space, the liberated life, the lightness – all of this will ultimately contribute to your ability to be productive. The comfort and support you'll receive will connect you with a sense of peacefulness.

Survivor Story

What helped you get through one more day?

There were many moments when my life felt simply dull and meaningless. I used to say I felt like I was wrapped in a cotton ball. I felt as if there was a distance between me and the beauty of life. As if I was in a very isolated, cold place, and all the beauty of life was somewhere else, and it felt like the distance was just so far. I felt disconnected from my purpose and from who I truly was. I didn't see myself.

What changed everything for me was discovering a spiritual path. I had to make some radical choices and remove myself from life as I knew it, remove myself from the familiar environment where I grew up, remove myself from my family, and go thousands of kilometers away. I ended up in the jungle in Thailand. I needed to go so far away to create a bit of a separation between me and the conditioning that I was brought up in. When I started to take deep breaths and meet people who were supporting me and guiding me back to me, for the first time in my life I felt the sense of home inside of me.

I had an experience that changed everything for me when I attended a silent meditation retreat in Thailand. I remember sitting there feeling so uncomfortable, feeling like my mind was like a monkey jumping up and down from branch to branch, from thought to thought. I was looking around at other people sitting there and they all looked like angels, in a blissful state, and I felt so inadequate.

But then, one day during a lunch break I was simply sitting there looking around when something profound took place. Suddenly I entered into a very special state. I started laughing and crying at the same time and I felt that I was flooded with light. It was such a profound experience. At that time, I'd never experienced anything like that. I felt like everything I've known myself to be wasn't there anymore. There was just this magnificent light. I knew myself as that light.

I don't know how long I spent in that state. It could have been minutes, or it could have been hours. But when I came out of it, I was a different person. I knew it was a one-way road from there on because I'd tasted my true nature. This taste isn't something that I could ever forget. That changed everything for me. That put me on the path that took me into experiences of my own limitlessness and seeing that I'm not conditioned by anything.

Survivor

Wherever you are on your path, know that no matter how dark it may look in some moments of life, these moments are simply part of being human. These moments are just that – *moments* – and they don't define the path of your supreme destiny. May you always find your way into a true place of truth, love, and infinite beauty. Because that's what it truly means to be human.

Connection

Your Own Circle First

Have you heard of Richard Branson, the British business entrepreneur? I first met Richard at a Halloween bonfire at his safari resort Ulusaba, where he was leading a Q&A session. My friend Natalie MacNeil had organized the trip and read out the questions submitted by the group. She asked Richard, 'What is the biggest opportunity or thing you think we can do for the future of the planet?'

Now, this is the guy who signed The Sex Pistols to his record label. He flew into space. He was one of *Time* magazine's 100 Most Influential People in the World. He's been knighted. So he knows a thing or two. Here was Richard's advice:

> *You have to look after your own circle first. Look after your own health and self. You can't change the world if you're not feeling good. Next, look after your family and friends, then extended family and neighbors. If everyone just did this one thing, the whole world would change.*

I found his words so powerful and I think of this advice often.

We have to look after ourselves and our own immediate circle first. We have to fill ourselves up – with self-love, exercise, healthy meals, relaxation practices that work for us, fun with friends, meaningful work. We can release the idea of being a martyr and we can release the idea that this work is a burden.

The work is, in fact, a gift! To ourselves and to others. Practicing the tools in this book is a joy! These tools are energy-giving, not energy-depleting, so whenever you need a little boost, pick up this book.

Things don't have to be complex to be true. That's a lesson I've been continually learning as I've made my way through challenges and harnessing the hope that Positive Psychology can bring into our lives.

Look after yourself. You're at the center of your circle – holding on to hope, practicing devotion, and connecting with others.

We Are Each Other's Medicine

Medicine is important. I wouldn't skip my daily supplements, and you know from other sections of this book that I don't skip exercise either. It's a positive habit I've built up over time, and now I do my best to walk and practice Kundalini daily, and run, hike, and do Pilates sessions weekly. Alongside my routine, I love working out with friends.

We truly are each other's medicine, so to maintain good mental health, it's super important to make time for friends. By thinking of your friends as the medicine they are, you can remind yourself to make time to connect with them every day. Research has linked having strong social bonds (or any social bonds) with lower levels of anxiety and depression, better well-being, and feeling more hopeful and optimistic about the future.[1] Vivek Murthy's book *Together* makes the case for loneliness as a public health concern, with unwanted solitude being shown to act as a negative amplifier of physical and mental health conditions.[2] And as I mentioned earlier, social support is closely tied to overall mental well-being.[3]

It's important to have one trusted person you can reach out to. While I haven't always been able to share my feelings with big groups of friends as openly and freely as I do now, what did feel possible when I was in a low place was to speak to *one* person and feel safe and supported within that relationship. You might feel a little vulnerable and uncertain about whether to share, how, and whom to share with. But every time I've shared within a safe space, it's felt like a huge relief energetically (even if what I'm sharing comes out in a way that doesn't make much sense until I talk it through.) Talking can help release some of the internal pressures, uplift you, and make you feel better.

What also worked for me was sharing gratitude with my friends, who would check in on me. I thanked them for caring and reminded them that I'm sometimes not the best at asking for help, so I invited them to continue to check in with me. This meant they felt better about reaching out and knew they weren't intruding or overstepping. I felt better because I didn't feel like I was being a burden by raising the conversation – it reminded me they cared and wanted to know how I was feeling.

Survivor Story

What helped you get through one more day?

I talked to someone who advised me [and] was able to give me solid facts as to why my depression was a normal reaction and why I wasn't imagining things in my life. I had a couple of unhealthy situations and relationships. They treated my case like an emergency because it was. They got me into a new living situation, and I got a job to support myself.

Survivor

Staying connected is an ongoing practice. I receive hundreds of notifications every day and yet sometimes, I don't feel like picking up my phone, let alone going to be social at an event.

Loneliness impacts our mental and physical health, and reduces our lifespan and our ability to cope. We're all still dealing with the fallout from the pandemic. At the same time, the pandemic had at least one positive impact: It opened up the conversation about mental wellness. A conversation once consigned to the sidelines is now mainstream. I also think it's helped us meet each other with more respect, peace, and compassion. Let's hold on to that.

Developing connections and positive relationships helps you strengthen your willingness to keep going, with social connectedness being shown to help prevent self-injurious thinking and behaviors.[4] Your relationships act as a buffer to any fear and stress you may be experiencing,[5] and even if you don't experience explicit emotional or practical assistance from people in your life, even just starting to notice you have relationships around you that feel good, or that you're part of a supportive social network, can reduce your experience of stress and help you feel more hopeful about the future as well.

In our One More Day framework, 'connection' is the circle that surrounds the others – 'devotion' and 'hope.' Connection with others is essential to the tapestry we're weaving. One of the simplest ways to connect? A conversation! Talking can improve your mood. A recent study showed that well-being can be enhanced by just *one* conversation a day.[6] I'm sure many of us have more than that, but the effect of even one is significant.

Let's commit to having more conversations. Pick up the phone. Step out the door. Talk with a neighbor. Meet a friend for lunch. And tag me in your photos on social media so we can celebrate building this new tapestry of social support together!

Eight Conversations to Feel More Alive

Here are some conversations you could have today. Pick one and give it a go!

1. A conversation with a trusted person where you feel supported and heard.

2. A conversation with someone who makes you laugh.

3. A conversation with someone who needs your support. Maybe start by asking: 'What can I do to support you right now?'

4. A conversation where you ask somebody about a favorite memory from growing up. Get curious. Discover more about them. What can you learn?

5. Find someone you're proud of, and tell them, 'I'm so proud of you.'

6. Ask someone about the best part of their day.

7. Follow up with someone and let them know how much you enjoyed getting the chance to talk or spend time together last time. These sentences are easy, but we often forget to say them:

    I really enjoyed our time together.

    I'm so happy we got to talk together.

    That made me feel good.

8. Ask someone what work they're doing that's exciting them at the moment. Or simply talk to them about the things they love doing. Maybe you can help them find more positive emotions and more meaning, and you'll be able to celebrate with them too.

Reflection

- Which prompt did you pick?

- How did you feel afterward?

- What did you learn?

- What was good about your conversation? Perhaps you're celebrating the accomplishment of attempting to have the conversation in the first place, or maybe there was something you enjoyed specifically that was said or noticed in how you felt.

- What conversation starter can you try next?

Positive communication leads to a positive feedback loop. A friend told me recently he was proud of me. It felt good in the moment and the happiness lingered into the evening when I remembered his words. It made me realize I wanted to circle back and let him know how much that meant to me. It made me feel so much better in my day, and he should know that. It also felt energizing to say that sentence to someone else and create a positive feedback loop.

The prompts in this section are for starting conversations to build our connections. But of course, many of you reading this book are also looking for ways to support loved ones who are struggling. So, it's important to be sensitive and mindful when thinking about what to say to someone who is having a hard time.

Most of us aren't experts, and it's our presence that will matter the most. Connection and belonging are essential to suicide prevention, and presence is its own kind of conversation.

Other People Matter

Who do you feel a connection with? Maybe it's a friend who makes you smile, someone who reaches out to ask how you're feeling, or that person who is always cheering you on. Maybe it's the neighbor you pass by once each week, a counselor, mentor, or coach. Remember, other people matter – positive emotional contagion *is* a thing, smiles are contagious, and even consuming positive content online is enough to induce the effect.

A study of 689,003 Facebook users[1] looked at whether emotional contagion only happens when people interact together directly or if we can experience the effect on our own. The experiment tested reducing the amount of emotional content in the news feed. It showed that when positive content was reduced, users created fewer positive posts and more negative posts, and vice versa when harmful content was reduced. This suggests that other people's emotions affect our own, and that emotional contagion is happening on a massive scale via social media without the need for in-person interaction. So, if you need an emotional boost today, connecting with *positive* content online can be a good thing.

We're all connected. There's always hope. If we stick together, there's always one more day.

And another.

And another.

Since 2022, I've been taking students through my PROMISE®
framework so they can experience a personal transformation and
get certified as Positive Psychology Coaches. That way, they can
use the tools within their coaching practice, role at work, family,
teams, and in their own lives. Each time we teach the Positive
Psychology Coach Academy Certification (PPCA), we have
students complete a validated well-being assessment and track the
'before' and 'after' data across 43 different scores to show the shift
they experience through taking the course. Every time, we see a
dramatic improvement in every measure of well-being. Belonging
and psychological safety scores always stand out to me.

Psychological safety focuses on how it feels to be part of a
community or group in relation to how comfortable you are
speaking your mind and sharing what you're thinking and
feeling. This variable is almost always the lowest score in the
community before the start of the course. Perhaps this is
related to all the changes and uncertainty we've experienced
in the world over the last few years. After taking PPCA, this
score improves massively, with students reporting feeling more
connected and like they belong in more places, including within
our online communities.

Even if we're used to complaining about the people in our lives,
positive relationships correlate with our ability to get through
one more day. When you realize the incredible power of Positive
Psychology to support a feeling of psychological safety and a
sense of belonging, it's clear to see how this science may help us
prevent suicide.

Finding Reasons to Live

- See the sunrise.

- Discover your purpose.

- Fulfill your potential.

- Inspire others through your story.

- Laugh so hard your stomach hurts.

- Enjoy the exhale on a deep breath.

- Feel the high after a workout.

- Help someone else via a random act of kindness.

- Hear the birds sing in the morning.

- Feel cozy inside when it's raining outside.

- Overcome a fear.

- Stare at the stars.

- Enjoy a hot meal.

- Go on a roller coaster.

- Listen to someone's old stories.

- Give (and receive) 20-second hugs.

- Orgasms (these appear on a lot of my lists!)

- Sing your favorite song loudly.

- Snuggle with your kids.

- Make a positive impact on someone else's life.

- Witness beauty in nature.

- Learn something new.

- Experience the awe and wonder in a child's eyes.

- Feel proud you kept going.

- Cherish memories.

- Feel a sense of belonging.

- Support others who need it.

- Realize it was worth harnessing hope.

- Remember your loved ones will miss you.

Now grab your journal and add some more reasons of your own.

I'm So Happy You're Still Here

One of the many amazing things I've found about writing *One More Day* is how much more connection is being created through conversations about mental health and prevention with the survivors and experts I've spoken to. I didn't realize how many of my close friends have been touched by suicide, with many having experienced suicidal thinking themselves. I've written about some of their stories throughout this book. I want to share another story here, as I figure the more examples of these simple and profound realizations and decisions to choose to live – or not to quit – I can give, the more hope you can feel that you, too, will see better days.

My friend Amber came to visit LA right before Christmas and we caught up for a drink with our friend Sahara (who had just moved back to LA as well) at one of the hotels on Sunset Boulevard. It always feels so good to have friends in town – like when you're a kid and you knock on your friend's front door down the street to see if they're playing out that day. We were chatting about what had been going well. As you know from earlier sections of this book, this is a question I love to ask. Even if it feels like everything is going wrong, when you shift your focus, you'll always find something good. I shared how I was loving the process of writing this book and how much joy and excitement it was bringing me.

Previously, Amber had been struggling with the loss of her dad and her beloved dog Angel, while supporting her boyfriend who had issues with addiction. Sinking under grief and tremendous pressure, she'd made a plan to take her own life. During this time, she was called into a Hollywood studio for the fifth time to audition for a presenter role. A fifth call back in Hollywood is apparently as good as getting the job. She was asked to write up and report on some gossip that appeared to attack a well-known singer. A short while before, Amber had had a fun night chatting and partying with that singer. It didn't feel good for her to then turn around and attack the young celebrity on camera. Amber walked off set, feeling the need for more purpose in her life. She told the producers she'd had enough, and she wasn't interested in being part of that character attack. 'I can't do this,' she told them. 'I'm not doing this anymore. My dad died, my dog died, and my boyfriend is struggling with addiction.'

As she exited the studio, one of the female producers stopped her, told her she shouldn't be on her own, and advised her to call someone. Amber played phone book roulette and flipped through her contacts, hitting the screen wherever it stopped, and calling a random friend.

It just so happened that the random friend she called was at a spirituality training workshop on the beach and had just been asked to nominate somebody to receive a free scholarship to study the spiritual degree. She'd chosen to nominate Amber and had written her name in the sand using a stick, so she couldn't believe her eyes when her phone rang, and it was Amber. She answered the phone, and they arranged to meet for a hike later that day. Instead of being alone and carrying out her plan to take her life, Amber now had a friend to spend the day with – and she also had *hope*.

When Amber told me this story, she described finding reasons to live as divine intervention. For everything to line up like it did, for Amber to phone that exact friend at the exact time she was writing her name in the sand – it was like the universe was calling.

Thinking about this powerful story later, I marveled at how it demonstrates both the power of listening to your intuition and the power of connection and caring for each other. Amber took a stand for herself that day, choosing to move forward with integrity and purpose. Then the producer had the foresight to tell her to call a friend, and it was that simple call to action which set the chain of events into motion that ultimately saved a life. Now Amber helps other people live their purpose and is both devoted to herself and her mission. Once again, I'm reminded of the seeds and the arrows metaphors – we don't always get to know who we help or how we help, but by doing a little bit for ourselves and each other, the positive ripple effect impacts in ways we might never see or know.

Name Five Things

During my darker days, sometimes I couldn't be bothered to take a walk to the fridge, never mind get up, get ready, go on a hike, and climb a mountain. I mean, I felt like I was climbing a mountain inside of my mind anyway, without even needing to go anywhere.

Recently, one of my friends was going through a stressful moment in her career, so we arranged to meet for a walk. When I arrived at her place, I found her distraught on the bathroom floor, shaking and sobbing. She was inconsolable. I knew straight away that there was no way she'd be up for leaving the house. In that moment, she wasn't even going to be able sit at the table and have a cup of tea. She didn't want to talk. She could barely catch her breath. Her nervous system was too activated. I needed something simple to be able to reach her.

I sat down next to her on the floor and said, 'Look around the room and name five things that begin with the letter T.' She looked around the room. 'Towel, tile, toothpaste, toilet, tap.'

This simple exercise brought her back to the present. She was in the 'now,' not in the catastrophic spiral she'd been in moments earlier. We hadn't solved anything about the challenges she faced. The problems were the same, but her breathing was more relaxed, her mind was no longer racing – she even laughed at how many things we could now see in this random bathroom that begin with the letter T!

When someone is that distraught, get them back to the present. Your job isn't to solve the problem. Your job isn't to make sure they immediately start doing a Positive Psychology intervention with proven benefits for enhancing mental wellness. Your job is simple. Bring them back to where they are.

Colors. Materials. Shapes. Name what you see.

Come Back to the Present

- Name five things you can see...
- Name four things you can hear...
- Name three things you can feel...
- Name two things you can taste...
- Name one thing you can smell...
- And finally, breathe...
- (And maybe even laugh!)

You don't have to wait for a friend to collapse on a bathroom floor. You can try this exercise with yourself as well. When you start downward spiraling into negativity, use this exercise to stop yourself.

Name three blue things.

Name three things made of glass.

Name three things made of stone.

And breathe.

Bearing Witness

One Friday, I received a text from my friend Leo saying: *Niyc, can you come get me?* It was unusual for him to send a message like that, and even though we'd loosely planned to maybe meet up, it felt like there was something more going on. I drove to pick him up and we headed to a restaurant. While we were chatting, he opened up about frustrations he was feeling around a struggle within his family ecosystem. I could see his anguish through his tears as he got up and went off to the restroom to gather himself.

As I waited for him to come back to our table, I thought about how we all have our unique version of suffering to master. What could I do for someone who was going through such a painful time? You can't wade in and give advice. And he hadn't asked me to, anyway.

I knew my friend was on his own journey. I've loved being on the journey alongside him as he opens up more deeply and navigates unfamiliar territory within himself. Our conversations are really special.

I realized we'd had about eight other deep conversations that had danced in this direction before he'd shared this element of what was going on for him. What I did throughout those conversations was continually hold space for him. I didn't judge. I didn't offer advice. I told him to ask me when he wanted support. I tried to stay steady. Be a friend. Listen. I asked what he felt he needed. And I made sure to continue to fill myself up.

I fill myself up so that if someone needs me, I can be there for them. And so that even if nobody needs my support, I've been there for myself. That's the ongoing nature of our work here – supporting ourselves, and then being ready to offer support to others. And allowing others to be there for us, too. Leo has been there for me. Solid, and I'm glad I can be that for him too.

I came across a meme I loved on Instagram that said: *Release the arrogance of wanting to wake up the other. You're not here to wake up others. You're here to wake up yourself.* When we remember to look after ourselves, we're more able to help others because of that.

I feel really thankful that my guy friends, as well as my girlfriends, open up to me about their mental health journeys, and about the therapeutic work they're doing for themselves. It feels so special to be in a world where men allow themselves to be vulnerable and supported. Growing up, I didn't see my dad shed a tear until my gran passed away, and that was when I was in my mid-twenties. So having so many men reach out to me now and share openly about how they're feeling feels like a big win, and like we're making some progress as a collective.

That Friday night when I picked Leo up, he was experiencing and sharing big emotions, and I understood that as a supporter, what may have helped create the space for this were all of our previous conversations. The showing up. And showing up again. Trusting each other. Vulnerable sharing. Non-judgmental listening. Patience. Not fixing. Honoring his presence. Honoring his story. We were gently walking the path. I knew my job was simply to listen and be present.

Leo said he hadn't allowed himself to feel his emotions in the past. He'd disassociated and distracted himself, consumed with work, movies, having fun, or the gym. He'd 'locked it away.' The feelings, the sadness, and the confusion. And when he started digging and doing the work, he let me know that for a while he was feeling worse than he'd felt in the past, when he'd kept the pain at bay.

My go-to trauma response had been to freeze, and I'd seen the trauma freeze response in front of my eyes with Leo, too. His eyes had glazed over mid-sentence, and he'd shut down. Usually, we'd have gone for a walk or an ice cream after dinner. But that night, he asked if it was all right for him to go straight home. Of course it was all right. I wanted him to do what he needed. We said goodbye and parted ways.

But as soon as I got into my car, I burst into tears. I felt grateful that I'd seen and understood the gravity of the situation, but I felt powerless to help him. Then I shifted from powerless to powerful. I remembered that presence is power, and I know just being there together was a tiny step forward on the path. For both of us.

Sometimes as a witness to pain, we feel helpless. But we may be forgetting how powerful a role we're playing just by being there. Allowing the grieving, releasing, and healing process to unfold.

Grief counselor Judith Johnson talks about the importance of 'bearing witness.' She offers the following advice: 'The focus is not to make the pain go away, but rather to let that person know that they're not alone and that we trust them to do whatever it is they need to do to go through that particular experience.'[1]

When you're called to listen to someone in deep distress, try to honor and trust in the other person's power and process. Truly listen and resist the temptation to offer advice based on your own map of the world. If you jump in with ideas about how to handle a situation, the person may retreat. They may stop being open to expressing what they're feeling.

Allow the person to feel. Give them a safe place to be. Provide support as the person allows the feelings to pass through their body. Give them a container.

I believe each person's soul has the strength to navigate and get through what they need to get through. What they need from us – the ones bearing witness – is to honor that internal light. That space where they can draw on their own intuition and personal power. Hold that person in their own knowing and power. Rather than offering advice, ask questions: *What has been supportive and working for you? What have you found helpful? What do you feel you need right now?*

This is the idea of 'holding space.' Being there. Listening. I know when my friends were supporting me through hard times, I really valued their presence. Hearing the words, 'You're doing a good job, Niyc' really helped me to keep going – even though I felt like I was doing a terrible job! Remember that positive emotions broaden your thinking, and help you build psychological resources and resilience. These keep you moving forward. This is how we'll all keep making our way through one more day.

It's so important to hold on to the energy of gentleness and patience. When you first hear that someone is having a hard time, it's natural to want to offer a way out. *Hey, I have something that might help you! Do it my way!* The problem is that the idea you suggest might not land in the right way. It can feel like you're not listening. Or worse, that you're bulldozing and talking about yourself, which can lead the other person to zone out completely and feel even more disconnected. If, however, you've made yourself available just to be a witness for someone, showing them that it's safe to feel, then you've opened a path for some practical advice that might be beneficial. But the first task is to assure them it's safe to feel. It doesn't feel safe when someone immediately offers a solution. Offer space and presence instead.

The answer here, as in so many places throughout our work, is to create more space for connection and conversation.

Survivor Story

What helped you get through one more day?

I read as many positive things as possible. I followed people who had changed their lives. I also attended a grief recovery course to deal with losses that I had experienced so that I could heal my broken heart and move forward.

Survivor

And remember, transformation isn't linear. This new social tapestry we're weaving is complex. We need a really big and forgiving loom. And lots and lots of time. We're going to have missed stitches. We're going to have long stretches where nothing seems to be taking shape. Eventually, we'll hold enough space and provide enough support to allow an upward spiral to birth.

Bearing witness. Holding space. These are powerful offerings. All you have to be is truly present for the other person. Your presence is the support they need.

Survivor Story

What helped you get through one more day?

Because of financial abuse, I couldn't afford a therapist straightaway. I went to a charity shop and bought a Tony Robbins book. During periods of anxiety and dark thoughts, I would open a page in the book and find something in the words to give me something to hold on to. A distant family member helped me with Neurolinguistic Programming (NLP), Cognitive Behavioral Therapy (CBT), and other positive coaching skills. I finally got therapy through my doctor. The counselor was a wonderful man who gave me skills to manage these dark thoughts.

Survivor

21 Ways You Can Hold Space

1. Ask someone to share. Be present. Simply listen.

2. Hold an intimate dinner party for people you know and love.

3. Help someone find a therapist.

4. Set up an accountability group.

5. Check in with yourself. Is there a way you can resource yourself right now so that you can be more present and effective at holding space for others?

6. Take a walk with someone.

7. Commit to making at least one phone call a day.

8. Ask someone how they like to communicate best (phone, text, WhatsApp, video call).

9. Let someone else start the conversation.

10. Ask someone to meet for coffee and bring your journals or sketchbooks.

11. Take a cue from my friend Danielle – call someone who has a super busy life but lives alone and say, 'What the fuck's going on in your crazy life right now? How are you really?'

12. Ring someone up in the late afternoon and ask them to come for dinner that night.

13. Ask if a video call could be an audio call and commit to using that extra energy you save for listening.

14. Go with the energy of curiosity rather than forcing.

15. Allow long pauses.

16. Make note of a phrase that makes you feel good and look for a place you can say it to someone else.

17. Accept not being able to fix everything. Let go of the need to.

18. Ask yourself, WAIT (Why Am I Talking?)

19. Hug without saying a thing.

20. Invite someone to co-work with you for an hour. Or co-read. Or co-watch!

21. Check in and ask someone, 'How are you feeling right now, on a scale of 1 to 10?'

Stretching Good Feelings

Time with friends is important to our mental health and well-being. Our connections and communities can bring us a great deal of hope and a sense of belonging, both of which are extremely protective against suicide. We also can extend the good feelings we get from time with friends by looking forward to positive plans and reflecting on them. In Positive Psychology, it's called 'stretching.' 'Savoring' is technically the correct term for this topic, but I'm going to stick with stretching.

So, what is stretching, exactly? Well, having a fun plan is, hopefully, going to be fun in and of itself. But looking *forward* to the plan can also bring joy. Do you have a hike planned? A concert? A visit to see a favorite friend or family member? A holiday dinner?

Anticipating these events generates a hopeful, positive feeling. We can extend our happiness by imagining the concert or the holiday dinner. What will you wear? Will you make something to bring to the dinner? Maybe try a new recipe? What's one thing you definitely want to do on your next vacation? All these thoughts can help stretch the joy that the fun event brings into our lives.

And stretching can go in the other direction as well, after the dinner or concert or vacation is over. We've talked in other places throughout the book about thinking about highlights from your morning or weekend. It certainly kicks off an uplifting conversation, but it also contributes to this stretching phenomenon, whereby you maximize the happiness in any given event. Looking back on photos, writing in your diary, telling a friend about the restaurant you loved, or the tropical fish you saw, or just the beautiful moon that lit up a dark October night – all of this will take the happiness you felt and spread it out further into your life.

There's another type of stretching I'd like to mention as well (still not yoga!), which is about getting outside of your comfort zone a bit. When we're trying something new, it's healthy to push ourselves a little, to stretch ourselves, but not to the extent that it would be overwhelming or debilitating. Maybe you'd like to join a walking group, but that sounds too intimidating right now. Why not stretch yourself, but gently? Call a neighbor and ask if they'd like to take a walk. You'll get fresh air, a little exercise, and some social connection – a three-for-one! Maybe in the future, you'll be able to increase that stretch and find a walking club to join.

Another way to think of this is as a sliding scale of edge. For example, perhaps the thought of eating in a restaurant alone feels scary. Personally, I love going out and eating on my own – people might think that's weird, but I highly recommend it. I always meet super interesting people this way. In fact, recently I met my Beverly Hills grandma, Gail, this way, and we've since had some amazing times together! Gail is a remarkable female entrepreneur and philanthropist in her seventies. When we first met, there was a moment when I teared up and thought of how much I'd love to be chatting with another young female entrepreneur when I'm in my seventies!

If eating out alone sounds overwhelming, start with stretching into a smaller edge. You could go for a coffee by yourself on a Saturday morning at a nearby café. Bring a book, a sketchbook, a magazine, or just yourself. People watch. Listen to the birds. Check in with yourself. Can you take a few deep breaths and feel more centered? Is it something you'd like to try again?

Perhaps going to the gym feels like too much of an edge. How about this instead: Set a timer to get out the door. Give yourself 15 minutes, and when the buzzer goes off, you need to have your shoes on and keys in your hand. Find a place where there are trees. That's it! I've said it in other places in this book, but it bears repeating: You only need to take small steps. Five minutes of walking five times throughout the day is going to be more manageable, and therefore more effective, than trying to do one long, hard workout that you never show up for.

So, even if it feels scary and hard – get started. Stretch into that edge and you'll feel better because of it!

Intentional Friendship

Many years ago, my friend Emily reached out to me and shared that she'd made a joy list: a list of all the people who brought her joy. I was on the list. She said she wanted to invest more time together in the year ahead, and really get more intentional about our friendship. I loved hearing this, and knowing that I was on my friend's joy list made me feel joy too!

What a lovely thing to hear, right? When you think about it, her words are another way of saying 'It's safe to feel.' Donna Ashworth, author of *Wild Hope*, offers some advice for finding your people. She says that when you meet them, 'It's a little fizz, a tiny little spark of something, that zips unseen between you. A soul recognizing another.'

Have you ever felt that? Almost an immediate sensation, your intuition saying: *This is someone I want as a friend.* Have you thought of telling the person? How might that feel, to verbalize your feelings, to put it out to the universe?

After that beautiful share from Emily, we continued to build our friendship, celebrate each other's high points, and support each other through challenges. Our growing relationship was a clear example of boosting well-being through connection and having people with whom we can be vulnerable. We might never have developed the depth of friendship we have right now if she wasn't so intentional about writing her joy list and reaching out.

Who would be on your joy list?

This also got me thinking about the intentional dimension of friendship. Not just the friendship itself – how well you relate, how much fun you have together – but whether you're *intentional* about making the effort.

This, in turn, prompted me to write a list (another list!) of all the people in my life who are intentional about their relationship with me. That is, those who actively make an effort to connect and grow the connection.

This exercise made me feel grateful for so many people. It also made me want to actively be intentional back and be proactive in fueling the positive relationships. It's a variation on our G-bombs (there are endless variations of being grateful, for which I'm super grateful!).

This exercise also got me thinking about how we can reverse engineer the path to suicide by taking 10 steps back from someone on the brink of wanting to take their own life, and thinking, what can we do *now*, when we still have so many options, to choose a different path?

One idea is to be more intentional about how we navigate our relationships.

A study in *Psychiatry* looked at the link between sense of belonging, depression, and suicide risk.[1] Participants, who were experiencing depression, completed interviews and assessments to measure depression, hopelessness, stress, social support, suicidal behaviors, and sense of belonging. The study found that there was a significant relationship between sense of belonging, depression, and hopelessness, which suggests belonging is likely to play a critical role in the development of depression, as well as in the recovery process. It also showed an indirect relationship between sense of belonging and suicidal ideation. This suggests that interventions, such as behavioral, interpersonal, cognitive, and those validated through Positive Psychology, may support the development of a sense of belonging, increase levels of hope, and decrease the incidence and symptoms of depression before someone gets to the point where they think about ending their life.

Relationships and being part of a community act as a buffer against stress. Receiving support and assistance from others increases our ability to cope. Though amazingly, the effect of lowering stress also happens even without other members of the community offering explicit help – just being part of something and knowing others are there can be enough to make a difference. People who have multiple strong relationships, and who are well integrated into society, are much less likely to die by suicide.

Increasing your sense of belonging begins with getting intentional about connecting with others. As well as looking for places to belong, let's also consider how we can create places for others to belong, too. Connection is another of my core values, and I love creating experiences for people to enjoy and feel included. For me, this looks like hosting dinners, leading my retreats around the world, running events, and building online communities.

Belonging Boosters List

Here's another list, specifically meant to help you get more connected with others. I want you to choose one thing from the list that you'll do today, and feel free to add your own entries to the list, too!

- Phone a friend or family member who helps you feel safe.
- Share your favorite funny meme with a friend through text or social media.
- Choose a memory that makes you smile and share it with someone.
- Ask someone what's exciting for them right now.
- Join a Facebook group and comment on someone's post in the group.
- Go to the store and speak with the staff at the checkout.
- Take a walk and smile at someone in the street.
- Reach out to a text-based mental health service like Talkspace.
- Do a random act of kindness for someone else.
- Host a dinner.
- Connect two friends who don't know each other yet.
- Sign up for a parkrun.
- Dabble in a new class or skill.
- Ask a friend where they feel they belong.
- Reach out to a friend and let them know you're there for them.

Think about building positive relationships as a process of making and nurturing bonds. People often ask me how I've had such great success in my coaching career. I believe it's because of the underlying psychological principles that run through everything I do. I build my business and teach in alignment with my core values of growth, generosity, and connection. Whether you're building a business or you're building a marriage, your relationships are at the core.

Survivor Story

What helped you get through one more day?

I found entrepreneurship and personal development. Two phrases that massively shifted things for me were 'Everything happens FOR me, not TO me,' and 'Everything always happens for my highest good in divine timing.' These helped me reclaim my power and believe that I had the power to create the life I wanted and change my circumstances.

Survivor

Meaningful Relationships Ritual

This exercise will help you get intentional about the relationships you have. It can be done with a partner, a friend, or even with a pet!

Step 1

Decide who you'll practice your Meaningful Relationships Ritual with.

Step 2

Take five minutes to write about your relationship with this person, or talk with them about all of the day-to-day things they do that make you appreciate and admire them. This can be as simple as saying, 'Thank you for stopping at the supermarket and picking up something for dinner. You're such a thoughtful and kind person,' or, 'I'm so grateful for the unconditional love my dog shows me, and how he makes me laugh when he races across the room chasing after his toy.'

Step 3

Reflect on how this exercise made you feel. Take a few moments to be in a grateful space and notice the positive feelings. Where there's more gratitude, there's less room for pain.

Step 4

Take out your alarm or your planner and schedule this exercise in for the same time tomorrow.

———————————

Developing connections and positive relationships helps you strengthen your willingness to keep on going. Even if you don't experience explicit emotional or practical assistance from the people in your life, just noticing that you have relationships around you that feel good, and that you're part of a supportive social network, can help you feel more hopeful about the future too. Your future is bright, and you're so, SO loved.

Join our free community and grab all of the resources from *One More Day* by visiting: www.niyc.com/tinytools.

Join in

I attended a business event with a peer group recently. I was a little nervous at first. In big groups, I usually hang back and listen, and I need time to recharge after being at social or business events like this.

I always love attending events in person instead of online – I feel like there's an extra texture and richness to the way we get to develop relationships in real life. Plus, I love taking time out from my normal schedule and routine, and getting my mind opened and stretched. By the time I head home I feel more clarity, inspiration, and a new wave of energy. I spend so much time coaching or teaching online, always thinking of the next thing to write for my books or say on social media. So it felt great to be nourished and filled up by the expansive conversations going on at this event, and I noticed a renewed sense of vitality and momentum too.

The trip reminded me of the importance of getting into conversations and rooms with people who have different skill sets, bigger mindsets, and alternative perspectives. I believe in always being a student and being curious about what we can learn. People who think bigger are doing bigger things.

Sometimes it takes a lot of energy to get into the room full of elevated consciousness. Every time before I travel, I still feel some resistance and wonder if I should just not go. How do we overcome resistance and jump into the expansion waiting for us?

Well, first of all, I want to remind you that you get to tune in to what feels right for you and ask yourself what you really need right now. There have been plenty of times when I actually didn't go to an event, because I knew I really needed to rest my body and mind instead. And that's OK, too. You get to do you!

When it comes to travel and being at events in person, I remind myself that fun is also a value of mine, and when we have more fun, we feel better and we're more successful. I also remind myself that a shake-up in my normal routine is valuable and nothing changes if nothing changes. I always trust that something cool will come from a new experience – and it always does.

Here's another reason to join in with uplifting, collaborative conversations – it's hard figuring things out alone. And we don't have to do it alone! Why not talk and figure things out together? Get creative, toss around new ideas, build off something someone else brings forward.

How can you get into a room where people are having expansive and uplifting conversations? Can you sign up for an event, a workshop, or a book club? Learn a new hobby. Make a list of your own strengths and teach something to other people. Engage. Be absorbed. Participate. Join in. Find something stimulating and invigorating. Go on a tour. Ask questions. Explore and discover. And remind yourself of what you love about the experiences you're feeling resistance toward.

Even though we know something is good for us, we don't always remember it, so I started to build systems and make checklists to help me get on track and make the most of it.

The Power of Pets

Love and connection with others doesn't always need to come in human form. One survivor that I spoke to said that her dogs started her healing journey for her. On days when she wanted to stay under the covers, she knew she had to get up and get moving for them. It makes sense – as well as providing connection, playfulness, and joy, a pet also provides purpose and helps you get up and out of the door on the days you might be finding it hard to motivate yourself to move.

Among the everyday challenges, there's a little bundle of unconditional affection that reminds you that you have something good to focus on, and that you're seen and loved.

Pets have a special way of providing comfort, purpose, and hope. Positive Psychology has studied their impact on mental health – we know that pets promote positive feelings like joy, gratitude, and love, and can increase feelings of companionship and attachment. There's also research that suggests the sensations associated with keeping a pet can snap you out of a downward spiral of thinking. I read a story about a woman who was planning to end her life and stopped because she felt her dog brush past her hand – the sensation was enough to bring her attention back to the present and remind her she was loved.

Survivor Story

What helped you get through one more day?

I had something to focus on other than my own pain. I had company. I felt safe. [My dogs] made me feel loved, which made me realize that I was LOVABLE, despite what my ex-husband said and did. And most importantly, they got me outside, walking and playing. I was terrified of people at the time – afraid that if the person I loved the most could hurt me so badly, how could I trust anyone else – so I took the dogs to remote forests, beaches, and trails. Sometimes on those walks, I'd feel the sun or the wind on my skin, and it would feel good. It would be the only thing that had felt good in days.

I started to look forward to those walks so that I could feel those moments. Those moments eventually opened up gratitude in me, and I consciously practiced more gratitude for more experiences. It helped me find the positives in life, rather than replaying my victim story over and over. My gratitude runs deepest when I think about my dogs because they were such an important part of my healing. For everything that they gave to me, I'm now dedicated to finding ways that I can heal them, creating healthier, happier, longer lives for all of us in a mutual cycle of positive energy and love.

Survivor

In the survivor story above, you can see how the connection and relationship with a pet can act as a gateway that has a domino effect into so many other positive practices. That rings true for so much of Positive Psychology, and for so many of the teachings within this book. Once you start one tiny thing, the other steps will feel easier to take from there – a natural progression, without feeling forced. This survivor describes feeling safe in her relationship with her dogs, which helped her experience more positive emotions like gratitude, trust, and love. They also helped her get moving and open up to the positive impacts we know come from physical activity, getting outside in nature, and the upward spiral of emotions and experience.

I've heard numerous stories like this from other survivors on my courses and on social media who attributed their recovery from suicidal thinking to the connection they had with other people or a pet.

Survivor Story

What helped you get through one more day?

A horse saved my life. I rescued him, but really, he rescued me. He's a four-legged Earth angel and a natural healer.

Survivor

If you don't have a pet, don't worry, there's lots of other ways you can build connections and strengthen your sense of belonging. Though sometimes when you're struggling, going out to social events and talking to lots of people may be the last thing you want to do. It's important to find connections in ways that feel good for you. Remember: Start by doing tiny things first!

Survivor Story

What helped you get through one more day?

My boyfriend and dog saved me. Bagel the beagle – his love was the love I felt even at my worst.

Survivor

The Mask

For so long I put on a front. Wore a mask. I'd pretend that everything was all right all the time. A shut-up-and-get-on-with-it kind of thing. Don't let anyone know the hard stuff. Smile and carry on.

And there's something to be said for the 'chin-up' approach to life. But not allowing myself to be vulnerable meant I didn't know what it was like to be deeply supported in relationships. I could talk about holding space and do it for others, but meanwhile, I didn't really allow myself to be held.

Even at times when I was really struggling with suicidal thinking, having a hard time just getting through the day, I wasn't able to communicate how I was feeling to my friends and family. It was already such an effort just to do normal things like show up for work and pretend everything was fine. The thought of then needing to explain myself to people just felt overwhelming when I was already completely exhausted. I felt like other people had enough on their plates and they didn't need to have my problems added on top of what they were already dealing with.

What I've learned though, is that we're hardwired to help each other. It's incredibly connecting when we're able to share our struggles and allow ourselves to be supported. Letting your guard down can feel scary sometimes. I didn't want to be a burden. So many times, I've been composed and put together on the outside, but terrified on the inside, just trying to make it through the day.

Many times, the universe had tried to teach me how important it is to allow yourself to be supported, but in the summer of 2021, I couldn't ignore the message any longer. I attended a spiritual ceremony where one of my best friends channeled a message for me.

'You need more support and holding.'

The words came out of her mouth in this slow, robotic voice. Her whole body was shaking.

The message continued:

'Allow yourself to be held and looked after. If you don't allow more support, you're always going to feel depleted. You have a big purpose on the planet, and you won't be able to live it unless you accept more holding.'

My friend talked about how I needed to seek out physical, mental, spiritual, and energetic support.

And then she was back in the room. Back in her body. The galactic voice was gone. Download received. Channel complete.

I knew I had to listen to that message. It was one of the most profound downloads I'd ever received, and I took it as a sign that I had to make a change. I absolutely had to take action.

Following that ceremony, I looked at all the areas of my life where I desired more holding and support and I assembled what I call my United Counsel of Support. (I made the name up and it makes me think of a team of helpful avengers!)

I already knew my friendships were present and evolved enough that I could be naked and real. It was my own evolution that needed to catch up, to allow myself to receive.

So, I finally told my friends, 'I haven't been feeling good.'

I could see their concern for me, which felt scary at first. It wasn't easy to be this open, but when I finally got the words out, it felt like this big exhale. It was a release of tension and such a relief that I didn't have to pretend everything was OK. Having someone bear witness and say, 'I can see you're struggling' – that felt really, really good.

Taking off the mask allowed my friends to see me and meet me in these conversations we were having. It required an energy of receiving, which, as I've said, isn't always easy. It served as an entry point for them to share more about what was going on in their lives, too. They were going through lots of difficult things as well.

Allowing myself to receive support and having these open conversations meant I could keep more of my energy. I didn't have to spend energy trying to make everything look perfect. Trying to keep up the mask.

Instead, I could look around and ask myself: What do I have in my life that's just for me? How can I look out for myself on all the different levels that my friend mentioned: physical, mental, spiritual, and energetic? What do I need for myself to be supported in these areas?

By opening up to receiving more help, I'd already made a start. I then made a list of where I could build a web of support: Hire a therapist, lean into relationships more, look to my existing mentors, hire a personal trainer, acknowledge my team.

Now I know some of these options aren't available for everyone. When I was looking for help back home in the UK, I was put on an eight-week waiting list to see a counselor. Sometimes resources aren't readily available when we need them. Let's take a Positive Psychology strengths-focused approach here and ask: What *can* you do? Where can you welcome more support? Which options are available? This book is a great tool you can add to your list.

The action I took was energized by the intention of receiving more support and being held more, and it felt powerfully transformative. My United Counsel of Support is still very much in place today.

Sometimes my friends and I ask each other, 'How are you, on a scale of 1 to 10?' The scale means that the person responding has to really lean into the question and think about how they're feeling. If they're not feeling good, it gives them a chance to communicate that.

This is a practice, like all the tools I'm offering in these pages. You don't have to share the biggest source of pain in your life right now with the next person who gives you a wave at the drugstore and asks, 'What's new?' – but be on the lookout for true, supportive friendships. Put energy into the relationships where you feel supported. And when it feels safe to do so, try opening up to someone who you trust.

Who might you want on your United Counsel of Support? Make a list and consider how you can take a step toward deepening the level of support you allow yourself to receive – and know that even by reading this book and allowing these words to support you, you're already taking action toward this!

Practice starting your conversations by saying, 'I'm really grateful I have you to talk to,' or, 'There's something I'd love to share with you today,' or, 'Can I share with you how I'm feeling today?' These are really simple conversation starters which open up the space without you needing to dive into talking about the way you're feeling right away. I really noticed the benefit of taking a breath and saying, 'There's something I need to say,' as sometimes it felt hard to just get it out, and I'd overthink it 89.7 million times!

When the people around you know you're struggling and you're open to talking, it means they're able to be there for you so much more. Being there for you might look like a daily text from a friend to see how you're feeling, or an accountability buddy who's checking in to make sure you did your daily walk. The idea is that you share your commitment to doing the tiny things, and they get to support you in doing them.

If you do give yourself the opportunity to be held by someone, notice how it feels. Perhaps it's scary at first, like it was for me, but eventually, there's a feeling of relief.

You're no longer carrying everything on your own. The challenges won't go away just because you share what you're carrying. But it'll feel a little bit lighter.

I feel a lot lighter in my life since I took off my protective armor. My friend Yossef came to teach a session at one of my retreats where students energetically removed their protective armor and it was so powerful! Yossef and I demoed the exercise, and I removed my protective armor of humor, which I use to laugh away tough stuff.

How does your armor show up? Perhaps it's through humor like me, or defensiveness, playing small, hiding, being extra brave, or being loud.

I consistently live the work – the radical self-honesty (even if it feels uncomfortable), the devotion to the Tiny Tools, to meditations, the steps outside, the chanting, the ice baths, the saunas – all the good things. When I'm having a tough week and things feel overwhelming or out of control, it can be easy to flip back to a negative mindset. So, I double down on the tools. They're simple, and they work. You just have to remember to use them.

Hope. Devotion. Connection. Every day.

Hard days and struggles can come and go. We don't reach a certain point where we've 'made it' and we're good forever more. It doesn't work like that. Some days will feel amazing. Other days will be tough. The difference is you now have tools to be able to cope better. Because as long as we're alive and we're holding on and we're harnessing hope, there's always one more day.

In our human experience, each day will have its obstacles. Obstacles we get to turn into opportunities. I live on mission. I know my purpose in this lifetime. And I know I'm a student again and again. Life is a lesson and a blessing all rolled into one.

Sometimes I have to just show the fuck up and get it done. Anyone who knows me knows I'm always open to learning something new and incorporating that into how I move forward. But when your mission is about connection, positivity, growth, up-leveling, momentum, I don't know, maybe it's easy to get caught up in that momentum and sometimes forget to look in the mirror at the end of the day and ask: *Are you OK?*

There's always another photo to take, student win to celebrate, motivating piece of copy to write. Sometimes I brush myself off, the way someone else might have brushed me off in the past. 'Stop being so ridiculous. You're fine, Niyc. What have you got to be worried about? Why on earth would you feel flat?'

Instead, what I really need to remember to do is breathe deeply for a few minutes. Or put on some music. Or meditate. Or chant. A tiny step. A gateway to feeling better.

I know that when I'm honest, when I'm real, and when I say, 'You know what, I'm not OK,' I get more connection, more growth, more community, more reasons to celebrate, and more momentum as well. Because being positive and everything being perfect all of the time just isn't real.

Reflection

- How are you feeling, on a scale of 1 to 10?

- How might you allow yourself to be held?

- What does it take for you to allow yourself to be supported?

- How can you open up the energy of receiving?

- What armor are you wearing right now?

- What was the highlight of your day?

- How did you make today work well despite challenges?

- What does your current support system look like?

- What more could you add to your support system?

Self-Forgiveness

I have a tendency to put a lot of pressure on myself. Even if it's on a really subtle level. I do this even though I know the research about the power of negative emotions and how they impact motivation and performance. Missteps, missed goals, moments when you want the ground to swallow you up, the times we didn't trust our intuition. It's easy to feel bad about ourselves for what we did or didn't do.

Are you ever unkind to yourself when something goes wrong? It might feel like you're giving yourself 'tough love' so you can do better next time, but, in fact, you might be depleting your own sense of confidence, and over time this can impact your motivation. We can get stuck in a low-level frequency, which makes things harder for us in the long-run. It's detrimental and self-defeating. You lose motivation, you stop taking steps, you stop seeing progress, and you stay in the negative loop.

Remember that negative thoughts and emotions are stronger than positive ones, so if you're telling yourself you're doing a terrible job over and over again, imagine the impact that's having on the way you feel generally.

For every time you're unkind to yourself about something, are you immediately telling yourself three good things you're proud of about yourself, too? No? I didn't think so. As well as boosting the positive, it's important to actively reduce the negative. Let's turn those subtle – or glaring – downward spirals into upward spirals instead.

It starts with self-forgiveness and a growth mindset.

'Self-forgiveness' might sound spiritual, or like a high-level idea, but it's actually quite practical. It's also super powerful and supportive of your motivation and willpower.

Researchers in Positive Psychology have paid considerable attention to the idea of forgiveness. The goal of forgiveness is to restore or increase the personal well-being of those who forgive. For those suffering or experiencing suicidal thoughts, self-forgiveness has been shown to positively impact willingness to live. It releases some of the internal pressure. I shared a story about writing myself a forgiveness letter earlier in the book (*see page 116*). Why not try this exercise yourself? It's something you can do again and again to help relieve tension and feel lighter.

When it comes to forgiving someone else, studies on forgiveness have shown that forgiving doesn't mean forgetting, condoning, pardoning, or excusing a transgression – and the goal of forgiveness isn't always reconciliation. Rather, forgiveness is something you do for yourself to release toxic negative emotions and reduce your level of psychological distress. The writer Elie Wiesel said that the opposite of love isn't hate, it's indifference. Hating someone takes just as much energy as loving them. The negative energy and emotion that you put into not forgiving can, over time, cause major negative health outcomes, and can perpetuate mental health decline. So, let's go in the opposite direction by embracing forgiveness.

Reflection

- Where could you practice self-forgiveness?

- Where could you give yourself more grace?

- How can you invite others to practice self-forgiveness too?

- How can you let people know they're doing a good job (maybe even a brilliant job)?

- How can you create an opening for people to recognize they're doing their best?

Learning from a book, you can grasp something intellectually and conceptually, but the change can't happen until you absorb the knowledge and put it into practice. That's when you truly learn. The embodiment and integration can lead to a shift, a breakthrough, maybe even a transformation. But it depends on lived experience. With our own lived experience of self-forgiveness, we can go out and teach it to someone else. You could be the source of that vibrancy in someone else's life.

Forgive yourself for wearing a mask for so long. Forgive yourself for feeling shame. Forgive yourself for missing your alarm. For skipping your workout. For taking a ridiculously long time to write up a weekly report because you kept checking social media. Or because you kept finding yourself looking in the fridge for inspiration! (Just me?)

In Kundalini, we say a blessing for ourselves, a blessing for someone who needs it, and a blessing for the world. If you're a source of power and light, you can pull from that energy to create positive change outward.

Positive Communities

Feeling like you're part of something is one of the main pillars of leading a flourishing life. On the other hand, feeling like you *don't* belong is a big risk factor for suicide. You can see the alignment here and the opportunity for the application of Positive Psychology to help prevent this risk. This could be one of the reasons that being locked up at home during the pandemic had such a negative impact upon mental health. We're social creatures, and we're hardwired for relationships. We evolve in groups and communities. We need each other, and we're more successful with each other, too. When we think about belonging in relation to suicide prevention, we quickly realize it's not a nice-to-have – it's a must-have.

So, what are you actually looking for when it comes to feeling like you belong? The theory of belonging teaches that human beings need to form and maintain positive, quality, and significant relationships with others.[1] The golden rule for feeling like you have places you belong is: frequently experiencing emotionally pleasant interactions with others, and interpersonal bonds or relationships that offer stability, affective concern, and continuation into the foreseeable future.

Essentially, people must believe that the other person in the relationship cares about their welfare and likes (or loves) them. Ideally, this concern is mutual so that each person experiences reciprocal feelings. When people don't experience this, it becomes a risk factor for suicide.

If we go back to the stories from earlier in the book, you'll remember I found a place to belong within the Kundalini community. I feel part of something, the teacher makes me laugh, we share smiles among the group, and even though I don't know everybody within the community personally, the consistency it's provided me with over the last decade is priceless. Knowing I could go to a class every day of the week if I wanted to, and knowing the intention of the practice is better health, greater awareness, and more personal connection, checks all of the criteria for a positive community within which I feel like I belong. I definitely feel better because of that.

The longest study on adult development conducted by Harvard University found that the strongest predictor of a long and happy life is whether individuals have quality relationships in their lives. As humans, we need love, and without it, we can't thrive. Without love, we'll live shorter lives, whether that's related to suicide or something else.

When we feel we have somewhere we belong – whether that's within a group community online, a tennis club in our local area, or with our family and friends – we're able to experience higher levels of self-esteem, greater satisfaction in life, faster recovery from illness, lower levels of stress, and a longer life expectancy.[2]

Where might you be able to find a positive community to be part of? Or perhaps reading this, you realize you're already part of one!

The Sloth and
the Unicorn

One of my happiest memories is of a visit to an amusement park. I'd taken the day off and my friends Kyle, Hiro, Jon, and I made the hour-long drive to Six Flags. We laughed so hard all the way. Long before I caught sight of the Twisted Colossus roller coaster rising above Magic Mountain Parkway in north LA, I was already having so much fun just being in the car with my friends. The boys asked about this book, and I happily jumped into sharing about the writing process and how much I was enjoying it. I was taking a break from work but feeling so connected with my purpose and finding so much joy in what I do.

We finally got to the park, and we had a blast on the rides, but the highlight of the day came from the sloth and the unicorn – which sounds like it's going to be a folktale with some deep, metaphorical meaning. (Take things slowly and believe in magic? Not bad advice, actually.) But the sloth and the unicorn were simply the stuffed toys we wanted to win. We were sitting in the burger joint in the amusement park when I caught sight of a coin-toss game and the cuddly toys lined up as prizes behind it. I was seized with the desire to win the fat unicorn and my friend Hiro wanted the sloth. As two grown adults, we told ourselves we were going to win the toys to give away as gifts for our friends' kids... even though I totally own that I really wanted to win it for myself!

We ran over to the game and started tossing coins, trying to get them to land on a plate. It was hilarious, and I wanted to win so bad. But the odds were stacked against us. For every five coins I threw, I might get one to land on the plate if I was lucky. I was feeling a little disheartened and like it would never work (remind you of life a bit sometimes?), plus it was a pay-to-play, and I was running out of cash. But we came together as a team – everybody persevered and cheered each other on until, right as we were about to run out of coins, the last one hit, and we had enough to win the unicorn AND the sloth! Sure, it took us a long time and a bunch of money before we won the two stuffed toys. But the vibe was everything! The thrill of the roller coasters was a rush, but it was the togetherness of that game and our friendship that really made my day. The good feeling – and us singing to Stevie Nicks in the car – carried me all the way home.

That day gave the four of us a chance to connect deeply in our friendships, learn more about each other, and enjoy the sense of well-being that came with sharing a fun experience. That night I was on a call with another friend, and we talked about the three highlights of our day. This conversation served as a kind of informal gratitude ritual, and the happiness stretched even further out as the bright sun of this long summer day finally made its descent in the sky.

We know from the research that being with others is healing and protective. Is there a place on your calendar you can schedule in something fun with a friend? Are there times in your week you can grab a chance to connect with a co-worker or neighbor? When you next meet with someone, can you start the conversation by asking about the highlight of their day (or week, or weekend)? Starting with a celebration or strength activates positive emotions and shifts you into a more open space within yourself and the conversation. The positivity boost means you build relationships more easily, plus you'll leave each other feeling good.

Maya Angelou said, 'At the end of the day, people won't remember what you said or did... they will remember the way you made them feel.'

Integrating what we know about the power of social connection to build resilience doesn't have to be challenging or feel academic. Like the other ideas in this book, these interventions are based on science, but in practice, my hope for you is that they can feel like an adventure. I invite you to be curious, embrace discovery, and revel in the possibilities. To look around and see if there's a giant metaphorical stuffed unicorn nearby, just waiting for you and a friend to try to win it.

Young People

Suicide is one of the leading causes of death in young people. I feel a responsibility to them. It's a big part of my mission to not just activate adults but to understand the ripple effect for our kids and future grandkids. A lot of people are talking about the impact of mental health on the next generation. We haven't yet seen the full extent and impact of the pandemic. A lot of children were isolated for a long stretch. How will that impact them in the future?

I'm also concerned about what social media is doing to a child's connection with their parents. And beyond that, to their connection with other human beings in social settings and to their connection with themselves. There's so much we can do to support kids in this space of growth and make sure they're getting the nourishing relationships necessary to a positive mental health trajectory. We need to talk to children about the way they're feeling. As a kid, I didn't have the coping skills I have today.

It's beyond fulfilling to see my students' children practice Positive Psychology tools and hear the stories of shifts in family dynamics because of the work a mother or father has been doing on themselves. It's the ripple effect in action, and a signal that this work facilitates generational change. If we can create a positive shift within the home, we can create a positive shift within the world.

How can we help children acquire the skills they need so they don't get to the point where they're desperate? By resourcing ourselves as adults first.

When I think about the ripple effect of Positive Psychology, I'm always drawn to the impact we get to have for generations to come. When we as adults can transform ourselves, we're able to impact our children and their children too – the potential is massive! What's important when it comes to boosting hope in kids is that they are excited about something meaningful in the future, can see multiple pathways to get there, and have help and support from an adult who is also hopeful.[1]

When my colleague Mel's daughter, Isla, was being bullied at school, she was fortunately able to walk a completely different path to the one I chose at that early age. Because Mel is well-versed in Positive Psychology – we affectionately call her 'Mel the Well' as she has an endless amount of knowledge and research to hand – she was able to be the caring, hopeful adult in Isla's life. She gave Isla tools to shift her thinking and perspective. Mel explained that hurt people hurt people and Isla was able to tap into compassion for the bullies and connect with her own personal power to rise above the experience.

Contagion

The more suicide is shown in the media and the more it becomes normalized, the more other people feel inclined to take their own lives, too. It's just one of the many frightening elements associated with suicide and it's shocking to see the phenomenon in action. My friend Karen told me about a spate of suicides that had taken place at her son's high school and although her story is tragic, it isn't unique – teenagers with friends or family members who have attempted suicide are three times more likely to attempt suicide themselves.[2] I've witnessed the phenomenon myself – losing three close friends and then countless more of our wider circle taking their lives too, I couldn't help but wonder if this was suicide contagion in action.

The good news is positive emotions are also contagious, and that's something worth remembering and orienting toward. A study of hope and suicide ideation conducted on students in the Philippines after the COVID-19 pandemic[3] showed that high levels of hope buffered against suicidal thinking, with hope being noted as developed via spiritual-based practices and support from hopeful parents and peers – all topics we've explored in *One More Day*. The more we can focus on expanding the impact of Positive Psychology, the more lives we can save.

Normalizing conversations about well-being and suicide prevention, along with more mainstream coverage in the media, can help raise awareness, prompt helpful discussions, and encourage people to seek help when they need it. Survivor stories about recovering from suicidal crisis can be incredibly helpful and have been linked to falls in suicide rates. It's important to maintain the focus on suicide *prevention*, to promote the positive contagion effect, and counter the suicide contagion effect unfortunately seen when the act of suicide itself becomes normalized.

Remember the ripple effect? It's real.

Keep Fighting

You're Fucking Doing This

I've made the commitment to pursue the mission of using Positive Psychology to help prevent suicide. But I've also given myself the time, care, and space I need so that I can show up to do this work as my best self. Are you giving yourself that, too?

When I experience immense challenges and stress, I feel like I'm underwater. It's like there's an energetic heaviness and weight hanging over me. Some people describe it as a dark cloud. It's a sense of having to wade through the day. Trying to catch a break. Trying to catch a breath. Trying to catch even the tiniest of vibes.

Not every day is going to feel easy. You don't have to feel happy all the time. The level of resilience and grit I've been able to develop is a gift, but it's not always easy. The energy of 'getting through' isn't the way I want to live my life most of the time – but it's a helpful energy to channel when you're dealing with tough stuff.

That's what we're asking people to do, right? That's what I'm asking you to do, what you're asking your loved ones to do. To continually choose to get through, even if they don't feel like it. Even when they feel like they can't. When it's not light, bright, and breezy – and let's face it, most of the time it's not.

Over the years I've handled a lot. I felt like I was running the gauntlet. I was just trying to get through hour by hour, barely functioning as I tried to keep everything stable among the chaos.

Even when life started to feel easier and I noticed a little relief, I still felt like I was running a marathon. It felt like it was one thing after another, and I wondered when it would get better.

I urge you to summon the energy of grit and resilience and keep taking steps to continue on the path even though it feels hard. Underneath, there's a deep level of trust and knowing that one day, everything's going to be better than ever before. And it will.

I want to be clear. I've written about living your happiest life within my first book, *Now Is Your Chance*, and I'm writing here about staying alive, but I'm also learning that getting into alignment can be *really fucking painful*. But it's worth it. It's essential. When you've been out of alignment, when you haven't listened to yourself, it's hard to find your way back.

Continually showing up is hard. Making sure every day that I'm being authentic in what I'm teaching and sharing takes a lot of energy. I've struggled my whole life with my own mindset and mental health, which is exactly why I know these tools do work. They're tested in the research, and I've tested them myself, too.

And as I move through life, I'm not always sharing all my shit in the process. I think there's something to be said for going through it and protecting your process, learning lessons, and finding silver linings. But it's also amazing to be able to reach for connection, share a reflection about what worked or what didn't, to point someone else toward where the gold can be found. Helping another person to learn something, discover an insight, or see themselves in my experience allows us both to garner growth.

I've had the shit kicked out of me again and again. I've been kidnapped, raped, bullied. I've lost seven friends, three of whom you know – Chris, Sara, Sophie – to suicide. I've been in an abusive relationship, been physically hurt, feared for my life. Any one of these experiences could have broken me at the time.

And in a way they did.

But I've put myself back together again and again. I've made a commitment to myself and to this work. To Positive Psychology. To Kundalini. To moving my body. To expressing my gratitude. To trauma work. To keeping my perspective. To harnessing my strengths. To leaning into friendships. To fight. To survive. To grow.

I made the pact with Sophie, and I've made a commitment to you, wherever you're reading this, that I'll sure as anything get to the gold hidden in the fractured bedrock under this rushing river where I'm trying to keep my head above water.

When I feel like giving up, when I just want to say, 'Fuck it, I'm not doing it anymore' – and trust me, I think that a lot – there's always a step I can take.

A sentence I can write.

A phone call I can make.

But then another thought comes into my head. *What happens if I do give up?* Well, I'm just going to have to start again. It's easier to keep going from where I am right now than to start again. What am I going to do, just stop? Give up on this mission?

NO.

I'm going to keep on going.

I want to connect you with that place, that fire inside: *I'm fucking doing this and I'm coming out the other end shining.*

A step you can take. A phone call you can make.

What if this became your mantra for one more day?

Maybe it's a little glimmer now, but that power is inside you.

You're reading this page right now for a reason. You have what you need to keep going. You have already done good things.

It's not going to be easy, but you have tools you can reach for. You have strengths you can draw on. You have people around you.

Start a conversation. Listen. Move your body. Laugh if you can.

You're fucking doing this. Fight.

Look How Far You've Come

'And I knew right then and there that I was never gonna let anyone get by me without understanding they might be hurting inside, you know. 'Cause life, it's hard. It's real hard.'

Ted Lasso

We tend to focus on what we haven't done yet. We get overwhelmed by all the items still on our to-do list. The looming (or maybe even missed) deadlines. The unopened mail. The upcoming appointments. It's heavy.

Part of having a growth mindset is taking the time to acknowledge and appreciate your growth. How can you have confidence that things will get better if you never take the time to look back and consider how many times they already did? You've gotten through tough times in your life already. You've got more resources now than you had then. You've grown a whole heck of a lot since then. Look how far you've come!

It's a process and it requires patience. Most things do. Looking at how far I've come gives me the confidence and trust that things will get better. There are options. This book is full of options, full of possibilities when you allow yourself to be supported.

Where in your life can you shift perspective, taking a moment to congratulate yourself on how far you've come, rather than fret about how much is left ahead of you? Have you made progress on a work goal? Started a new hobby? Organized your home or workspace? Tried a new exercise routine? Broken out of a bad habit? Started a good one?

What's on your list of awesome things about you?

Positive Vision

When we create a positive vision for ourselves, we can align our current actions with what we'd like people to say about us in the future. This exercise can help you define your core personal values so that you can stay true to them as you go through life.

- Consider the future version of yourself – perhaps in 5, 10, or 15 years' time.

- What qualities do you want others to celebrate about you?

- If you were a fly on the wall listening to your friends talking about you (like a positive version of gossiping behind your back!), what would you like them to be saying?

- How would you like to be spending your time?

- Take as much time as you need to answer these questions, then consider how you might embody the characteristics of your future self.

- Take a step toward creating your positive vision today.

The Optimist Creed

My gran had a framed copy of Christian D. Larson's *The Optimist Creed* on her wall. I've always loved it:

Promise yourself:

To be so strong that nothing can disturb your peace of mind.

To talk health, happiness, and prosperity to every person you meet.

To make all your friends feel that there is something in them.

To look at the sunny side of everything and make your optimism come true.

To think only of the best, to work only for the best, and to expect only the best.

To be just as enthusiastic about the success of others as you are about your own.

To forget the mistakes of the past and press on to the greater achievements of the future.

To wear a cheerful countenance at all times and give every living creature you meet a smile.

To give so much time to the improvement of yourself that you have no time to criticize others.

To be too large for worry, too noble for anger, too strong for fear, and too happy to permit the presence of trouble.[1]

Accept New Versions

Part of getting to know ourselves, and learning to look after ourselves, is accepting that we're continuously changing.

I've learned so much in the past decade about how I want to structure my life, but if my daily routine 10 years ago looked the way it does today, I'd never have created the success I'm creating now. We're moving through different versions of ourselves, ever evolving in a spiral, not a direct line. Sometimes progress is fast. Sometimes it's full of setbacks. There are snakes and ladders. Obstacles that will pull us off course. It's not easy, this process of feeling, listening to ourselves, learning, shifting, adjusting, and re-adjusting.

But it's being alive.

This Book Is Alive

I was in Las Vegas when I handed in the first draft of this manuscript to my editor. I was there to see the Formula 1 race – a dream of mine since I was a little girl. It was such a full-circle moment for me, filled with memories of Sunday mornings spent with my dad reading *The Times* newspaper with a bacon sandwich and the Grand Prix on the TV. I grew up thinking the Grand Prix was just for rich people, and that I'd only ever be able to watch it on TV. Years later, I let go of my idea of a career as a mechanical and automotive engineer to study psychology instead, based on a single conversation which intuitively guided me toward this aligned journey of helping people feel better more of the time through my work. So, being at a race in Las Vegas and also hitting send on the email for this book made me realize how much flows into your life when you follow your intuition and make decisions born from contribution and purpose.

What happened next felt even more special. After sending the manuscript off, I headed out to the race with our group – I was the only woman in the main group of 12. The guys celebrated me finally joining them and when we were in the taxi, they asked me what my book was about. Again, I was presented with a beautiful opening for so many rich conversations, which lasted across the next few days, this time including men's mental health.

As we got out of the taxi, one of the guys shared with me that he'd experienced suicidal thinking a few years back. What snapped him out of the way he was feeling was something so incredibly simple. He was scrolling on social media when a positive quote jumped out at him. He said it was something like, 'Change your mindset, change your life.' What I love about his story is that it shows how powerful positive words can be. It doesn't need to be groundbreaking or be rocket science to be effective. Words will land right at the time they're meant to.

Putting out positive words, both verbally and on social media, can really help others. This man was struggling, and the quote he saw sparked something that motivated him to start to change his mindset. He's now happy, successful, and most importantly, still here to share his story.

Survivor Story

What helped you get through one more day?

I think it was a mixture of things, really. The National Society for the Prevention of Cruelty to Children (NSPCC) helped me. Their support groups and therapy sessions. Also my nan's words: 'You can do anything you want if you put your mind to it.'

My nan was my queen. She had no idea how bad things were at home, nor how bad things got when I was alone. I didn't want to break her heart, so I kept everything from her. She's the reason I didn't end my life.

Survivor

Throughout this past year of writing, many conversations and events have found their way into this book. New lessons were continually reshaping it, helping me to make connections between my research and experience. While I was generating material for the early drafts of *One More Day*, I realized I could do that walking outside in my neighborhood. So, I was able to apply a Positive Psychology intervention literally through the creation of this book, by getting outside and into nature.

That's what I mean when I say this isn't just a proven science, it's a way of life. There have been so many moments where I've felt the universe guiding me.

As I pour my heart out here, I refill myself with my purpose. My devotional practice.

I hold on to a feeling of hope.

You sometimes see people shut down when the topic of suicide comes up, and here I am talking about it daily, and I feel great.

This book is alive, I think, every time I sit down to work on it. And when I'm not sitting down to work on it, it's on my mind, it's in my steps. I'm part of the tapestry. From every direction, it comes at me. A comment on an Instagram post. A last-minute trip to see friends from home. There's a current running through my life and onto these pages.

I know the research supports these methods for shifting mood and even keeping people alive, but I didn't know the work itself would have this energetic property.

When I first started working on this topic, I wondered if I needed to schedule therapy sessions after each writing session to make sure I'd be OK during this process. Talking about my friends who have taken their own lives and sharing my own struggles – it was bringing so much forward. But it turned out that I'd leave each writing session feeling high and happy. This writing is my therapy.

This book isn't a challenging conversation for me. It's the opposite. It's exciting, uplifting. It makes me feel more connected with you, the reader, and with the world. Writing about my friends keeps them present with me, and, as much as I miss them, that lifts me up as well.

I hope that as you're reading, you're also noticing things in your life that spark a memory or a new point of view. A reason to be grateful. A new lesson. Maybe it's a tree branch, a snippet of a poem, a voice that reminds you of someone from long ago.

Your growth is at the center of this work. When you opened these pages you accepted the call and began a new journey. You belong here. You're important to this work.

Reflection

Spend time thinking about the following questions:

- What are you seeing and hearing in your life that relates to the ideas presented in this book?

- What synchronicities or coincidences are you noticing?

- When has a walk felt both real and symbolic, like you're traveling somewhere mentally as well as physically?

- What are you learning?

- What are you wondering?

- What positive step forward can you take?

It's Up to You

You're almost through reading the book.

I hope by now it's clear that, to impact your life, Positive Psychology has to become a way of life, not just a topic you read about once. This is a good opportunity to mention the person-activity fit. This is a concept within Positive Psychology that teaches that different interventions are going to work better and be enjoyed more by different people.

It's important for anyone who is struggling, as well as gatekeepers, to understand that Positive Suicidology isn't a one-size-fits-all approach. Some people respond better to strenuous workouts and others to gentle meditation. The more compassion and flexibility you have for yourself, the more you'll be able to help yourself and others. Some exercises and interventions in this book are likely to be hard for you. Others will feel natural. Others still might become more enjoyable over time.

My invitation to you is to try them all. Try them all more than once. Keep a note of how you feel. Keep it simple – make a note in your journal or phone about your experience and notice, step by step, which exercises you enjoy the most.

Keep Going

Giving up isn't glorious. It isn't glamorous.

There's a better way.

One filled with hope.

One filled with help.

One filled with power.

You'll be OK.

You're important.

Life is worth it. Life is precious.

Stay.

Keep it simple. Take a step.

Talk with someone.

Harness hope.

Choose devotion.

Find connection.

Keep going. One More Day.

A Girl from Newcastle

What about that 11-year-old girl, little Nicola, who was so afraid to go to school that she felt that giving up her life was a better option than facing the bullies for another day. That little girl was terrified. Scared for her physical safety and so uncomfortable in her body.

Early adolescence is an awkward time. Eleven-year-old Nicola didn't feel confident like I do now. I didn't feel a sense of personal power and I had no idea how to develop one. I didn't have coping skills. I'd told my parents a little about what was happening, and they'd spoken to the teachers. My teacher had even changed my class, which meant I wasn't in the same group as the bullies anymore. But that wasn't enough. That didn't change the way I felt.

I never really talked to anyone about what I was feeling. No one said, *Let's talk through what you're thinking about, what you're feeling in your body. Let's write down everything you're scared of, Niyc.* Instead, I was just told that everything would be OK. That I shouldn't worry about the bullies. Don't let them get to you.

But I didn't know *how* to stop it from getting to me. I didn't have the tools to know what to do, and my teachers and my parents didn't have them, either. I don't blame them. So much of what I can capture here has come out of new research and new understandings about resilience and protective factors in preventing suicide. As humans generally, we're facing a difficult moment. Children now have so much pressure on them. Academic pressure. Economic pressure. Climate change weighs on their minds. Many are stressed and anxious every day – and that's before we add social media into the mix....

But we also live in an amazing time. A time when there's so much awareness about mental health. Every day I wrestle with questions about life and death. What we can do to choose life for ourselves, and make sure others we love make that same choice. What kind of routines can center us and keep us hopeful. I pore over the research about what can save us. I attend conferences. I interview experts. I read the latest studies. Yet I can't say I know the full story of that young girl in Newcastle, or what happens in her next chapter.

I do know that her grandmother Mary volunteered for the Samaritans for so many decades that she was awarded a certificate for long service. When someone who was on the verge of taking their own life called, Gran would answer. She was present for these strangers in their most desperate moments. Gran was also there when someone felt alone and just needed someone to talk to. You don't need to be in crisis to call a hotline like the Samaritans. In fact, 75% of calls are not crisis calls at all.

I do know that 25 years after her suicide attempt, little Nicola – whose name means 'victory for the people' – had become a Positive Psychologist writing a book about suicide prevention, blessed with the opportunity to share that message with you.

I had to write this book. This was what I was born to do and what I stayed alive to do.

I'm here. And I'm doing my best to be as present as possible for as many moments as I can. Writing this book has helped me process my life and further refine my purpose. I've absolutely LOVED this process. I know that the topic of suicide prevention can be hard to discuss, but I also believe the conversation can be inspiring, uplifting, joyful, and energizing. Love within grief, energy within loss, purpose within pain, my joy-filled contribution to new energy for the world.

I stayed here and got to where I am now – living a life that others don't have – by working my ass off for two decades, sacrificing, and doing things other people wouldn't do. It wasn't handed to me, but I accept the responsibility it now gives me, and I know I can make a difference for others. I can link my arms with yours and encourage you to link yours with someone else's. I can spark conversations that will bring excitement and joy to an area filled with so much confusion and devastation.

I've been in many shitty situations. So many times, I've thought, *Oh fuck, how am I gonna get through this?* Sometimes, I'm on top of the world, and sometimes, even now, the journey can be very lonely.

But I always come back to who I am, remembering what I got through in the past, remembering everything is always temporary. I'm a girl from Newcastle who is gritty as fuck, resilient as fuck, who is able to hear a song that reminds me of a dear friend who left this world too soon, and still see the beauty through the tears.

Sometimes, even now, I've wondered, *What if I just wasn't here?* Unfortunately, that pattern is in my brain. The thought has already been imprinted into the way I think, but it's met, and batted back, each time now with a more powerful thought: *I have too much to offer the world to ever take my own life.*

The same is true for you or your loved ones who are struggling. If you don't know your meaning and purpose yet, it means it's still out there, waiting to be discovered. Could anything be more hopeful?

I don't know my soul's entire journey, but I do know it couldn't have a plot twist like me taking my own life. Imagine the headline:

AUTHOR WRITING ABOUT SUICIDE PREVENTION TAKES HER OWN LIFE.

That's not an option. I've got so much work to do on this planet. That can't be my soul's purpose.

Taking your own life can't be your soul's purpose, either.

For some years before we lost her, my friend Sophie would tend my grandmother Mary's grave, as her apartment overlooked the cemetery. 'I'll keep an eye on her for you, Niyc,' she'd say.

Thank you, Sophie, for tending to my grandmother after she passed. Thank you, Gran, for answering the phone when desperate souls called, offering them a way to stay living long enough to see the morning light. It was love, pure love, you gave to me and others, and I hope I've been able to bring it forward through the pages of this book.

I'm still here. Planting seeds. Shooting arrows.

And I know you're here with me, too.

Recommended Reading

Bryan, C. J. (2022), *Rethinking Suicide: Why Prevention Fails, and How We Can Do Better*. New York: Oxford University Press.

Hirsch, J., Chang, E., and Kelliher Rabon, J. (2019), *A Positive Psychological Approach to Suicide: Theory, Research and Prevention*. Cham: Springer.

Redfield Jamison, K. (2000), *Night Falls Fast: Understanding Suicide*. New York: Vintage Books.

Yu Moutier, C., Pisani, A. R., and Stahl, S. M (2021), *Suicide Prevention: Stahl's Handbooks*. Cambridge: Cambridge University Press.

Resources

Wherever you are in the world, help is available. Here is a list of places you can reach out to if you need support. Many of these resources have webchat and text options if you don't feel comfortable talking on the phone.

International
Befrienders Worldwide
- https://befrienders.org/

Find a helpline
- https://findahelpline.com/

United States of America
988 Suicide & Crisis Lifeline
- https://988lifeline.org/
- Call or text 988

Crisis Text Line
- https://www.crisistextline.org/
- Text 'HOME' to 741741

Trevor Lifeline
- https://www.thetrevorproject.org/
- Call 1-866-488-7386
- Text 'START' to 678678

Veterans Crisis Line

- https://www.veteranscrisisline.net/
- Call 988 then press 1
- Text 838255

Trans Lifeline

- https://translifeline.org/
- Call 877-565-8860

United Kingdom

Samaritans UK

- https://www.samaritans.org/
- Call 116-123

SOS Silence of Suicide

- https://sossilenceofsuicide.org/
- Call 0808-115-1505

Shout Crisis Text Line

- https://giveusashout.org/
- Text 'SHOUT' to 85258

Campaign Against Living Miserably (CALM)

- https://www.thecalmzone.net/
- Call 0800-58-58-58

Papyrus Prevention of Young Suicide HOPELINE247

- https://www.papyrus-uk.org/papyrus-HOPELINE247/
- Call 0800-068-41-41
- Text 07860-039-067

Canada

988: Suicide Crisis Helpline

- https://988.ca/
- Call or text 9-8-8

Kids Help Phone

- https://kidshelpphone.ca/
- Call 1-800-668-6868
- Text 'CONNECT' to 686868

Hope for Wellness

- https://www.hopeforwellness.ca/
- Call 1-855-242-3310

Trans Lifeline

- https://translifeline.org/
- Call 877-330-6366

Australia

Lifeline

- https://www.lifeline.org.au/
- Call 13-11-14
- Text 0477-13-11-14

Suicide Call Back Service

- https://www.suicidecallbackservice.org.au/
- Call 1300-659-467

Beyond Blue

- https://www.beyondblue.org.au/
- Call 1300-22-4636

MensLine Australia

- https://mensline.org.au/
- Call 1300-78-99-78

13 Yarn

- https://www.13yarn.org.au/
- Call 13-92-76

Acknowledgments

Thank you to my publisher Hay House, to Amy Kiberd, Michelle Pilley, and Reid Tracy, for believing in the message of this book, and for believing in me to be the person to write and share it.

To my editor Grace Rahman, my writing partner Rachel Federman, and everybody in my Hay House team. Working on this book together has brought me so much joy! I'm deeply grateful for your support and spirit, and I'm excited for the positive ripples to reach far and wide.

To Kyle Gray, for seeing me, for seeing this soul mission, and for energizing this journey with me. Your insight, support, and strength mean more than you know.

To Kelly Notaras, for being a stand for my message, for this book, and for holding space for me. I'll always remember the exact moment the title for *One More Day* dropped in during our call.

To Louise Hay, who I still listen to every day. Thank you for your vision and for creating a space for us to continue your legacy and help build a better world through our work.

To the Samaritans, for reading this manuscript.

To Gran, for showing me lives can be saved.

To Corey Kupfer, Danielle Canty, Darrius Marcellin, Dr. Erin Haskell, Natalie MacNeil, Maggie Colette, Orit Mesica, Rha Goddess, Yossef Sagi, for seeing me, supporting me, fighting for me, and helping me fight for myself when I felt I had nothing left. Thank you for saving my life.

To Ali Machedon and Melanie Deague, for standing with me, for your unwavering love and loyalty, and for being on this wild journey with me – armed with Positive Psychology tools to weather all storms.

To Jamie Freed, for your support, strength, guidance, and for believing in me and my work in the world, and here in the US.

To my family, my team, my dear, dear friends, and all who have contributed to the journey of *One More Day* and the stories within this book – Alyssa, Amber, Ange, Anna, Ashley, Bry, Chris, Caroline, Giulia, Gry, Jerry, Jade, Koya, Laura, Lola, Sahara, Sarah, Sarah, Tatiana, Travis, Will – I'm deeply grateful every day to belong in relationships that feel like home.

To everybody who has rallied around me to support this important work. Thank you for standing with me. Thank you for helping me save lives.

References

Seeds

1. Pidgeon, N. (2017), *Now Is Your Chance: A 30-Day Guide to Living Your Happiest Life Using Positive Psychology*. London: Hay House.

2. Bryan, C. J. (2022), *Rethinking Suicide: Why Prevention Fails and How We Can Do Better*. New York: Oxford University Press.

3. *Ibid.*

Welcome

1. https://www.who.int/news-room/fact-sheets/detail/suicide [Accessed 14 May 2024]

2. Cerel, J., et al. (2019), 'How Many People Are Exposed to Suicide? Not Six', *Suicide and Life – Threatening Behavior*, 49(2): 529–534.

3. O'Hara, D. (2013), *Hope in Counselling and Psychotherapy*. London: Sage Publications; Snyder, C. R., et al. (1991), 'The will and the ways: Development and validation of an individual-differences measure of hope', *Journal of Personality and Social Psychology*, 60(4): 570–585.

4. Harmer, B., et al. (2024), 'Suicidal Ideation' [updated 14 January 2024]. In: StatPearls [Internet]. Treasure Island (FL): StatPearls Publishing; 2024 Jan. Available at https://www.ncbi.nlm.nih.gov/books/NBK565877/. [Accessed 15 May 2024]

The Ripple

1. O'Connor, S. and Cavanagh, M. (2013), 'The coaching ripple effect: The effects of developmental coaching on wellbeing across organisational networks', *Psychology of Well-Being: Theory, Research and Practice*, 3(1): 2.

2. Barsade, S. G. (2002), 'The Ripple Effect: Emotional Contagion and Its Influence on Group Behavior', *Administrative Science Quarterly*, 47(4): 644–75.

3. Fetell Lee, I. (2018), *Joyful: The Surprising Power of Ordinary Things to Create Extraordinary Happiness*. London: Rider.

Tiny Tools

1. A literature review published in 2004 in *The Journal of Psychiatric and Mental Health Nursing* found exercise 'reduces anxiety, depression, and negative mood, and improves self-esteem and cognitive functioning.' See: Callaghan, P. (2004), 'Exercise: a neglected intervention in mental health care?', *Journal of Psychiatric and Mental Health Nursing*, 11(4): 476–83.

2. Edwards, M. K. and Loprinzi, P. D. (2018), 'Experimental effects of brief, single bouts of walking and meditation on mood profile in young adults', *Health Promotion Perspectives*, 8(3): 171–78.

3. Singh, B., et al. (2023). 'Effectiveness of physical activity interventions for improving depression, anxiety and distress: An overview of systematic reviews', *British Journal of Sports Medicine*, 57(18): 1203–1209.

4. Choi, K. W., et al. (2020), 'An Exposure-Wide and Mendelian Randomization Approach to Identifying Modifiable Factors for the Prevention of Depression', *The American Journal of Psychiatry*, 177(10): 944–54.

5. Haghighatdoost, F., et al. (2018), 'Drinking plain water is associated with decreased risk of depression and anxiety in adults: Results from a large cross-sectional study', *World Journal of Psychiatry*, 8(3): pp.88–96.

6. Walsh L. C., et al. (2022), 'What is the Optimal Way to Give Thanks? Comparing the Effects of Gratitude Expressed Privately, One-to-One via Text, or Publicly on Social Media', *Affect Sci.* 4(1): 82-91.

7. Kelly, J. S. and Bird, E. (2021), 'Improved mood following a single immersion in cold water', *Lifestyle Medicine*, 3(1): 1–9.

8. Shevchuk, N. A. (2008), 'Adapted cold shower as a potential treatment for depression', *Medical Hypotheses*, 70(5): 995–1001; Mooventhan, A. and Nivethitha, L. (2014), 'Scientific Evidence-Based Effects of

Grow Through What You Go Through

1. World Health Organization (1992), 'The ICD-10 Classification of Mental and Behavioural Disorders: Clinical Descriptions and Diagnostic Guidelines': https://www.who.int/publications/i/item/9241544228. [Accessed 14 May 2024].

237

2. Fox, V., et al. (2021), 'Suicide risk in people with post-traumatic stress disorder: A cohort study of 3.1 million people in Sweden', *Journal of Affective Disorders*, 279: 609–616.

3. Tedeschi, R. G. and Calhoun, L. G. (1996), 'The Posttraumatic Growth Inventory: Measuring the positive legacy of trauma', *Journal of Traumatic Stress*, 9(3): 455–71.

4. Bush, N. E., et al. (2011), 'Posttraumatic growth as protection against suicidal ideation after deployment and combat exposure', *Military Medicine*, 176(11): 1215–22.

5. Tedeschi, R. G., et al. (2018), *Posttraumatic growth: Theory, research, and applications*. London: Routledge.

6. Levi-Belz, Y., et al. (2021), 'Turning personal tragedy into triumph: A systematic review and meta-analysis of studies on posttraumatic growth among suicide-loss survivors', *Psychological Trauma: Theory, Research, Practice, and Policy*, 13(3): 322.

Noticing

1. Schmelefske, E., et al. (2022), 'The Effects of Mindfulness-Based Interventions on Suicide Outcomes: A Meta-Analysis', *Archives of Suicide Research*, 26(2): 447-464.

2. Luoma, J. B., & Villatte, J. L. (2012), 'Mindfulness in the Treatment of Suicidal Individuals', *Cognitive and Behavioral Practice*, 19(2): 265–276.

The Power of Positive Environments

1. Seligman, M. E. P. (2011), *Flourish: A Visionary New Understanding of Happiness and Well-Being – and How to Achieve Them*. London: Nicholas Brealey Publishing; Donaldson S. I., et al. (2022) 'PERMA+4: A Framework for Work-Related Wellbeing, Performance, and Positive Organizational Psychology 2.0.' *Frontiers in Psychology* 12: 817244. doi: 10.3389/fpsyg.2021.817244

2. Oh, K. H., et al. (2020), 'Six-Step Model of Nature-Based Therapy Process', *International Journal of Environmental Research and Public Health*, 17(3): 685.

Raising Our Voices

1. Suicide Prevention Services of America: https://www.spsamerica.org/facts-about- suicide/. [Accessed 14 May 2024].

2. Ivey-Stephenson, A.Z., et al. (2020), 'Suicidal Ideation and Behaviors Among High School Students – Youth Risk Behavior Survey, United States, 2019', CDC *MMWR*, 69(1): 2019 Youth Behavior Risk Survey.

3. Bridge, J. A., et al. (2018), 'Age-Related Racial Disparity in Suicide Rates Among US Youths From 2001 Through 2015', *JAMA Pediatrics*, 172(7): 697–99; Caron, C. (2021), 'What's Going on With Our Black Girls?' Experts Warn of Rising Suicide Rates', *The New York Times*: https://www.nytimes.com/2021/09/10/well/mind/suicide-rates-black-girls.html [Accessed 20 October 2023].

4. Black Mental Health: What You Need To Know: https://www.mcleanhospital.org/essential/black-mental-health#:~:text=Black%20people%20are%20far%20less,major%20contributor%20to%20this%20disparity. [Accessed 14 May 2024].

5. AACAP Policy Statement on Increased Suicide Among Black Youth in the U.S.: https://www.aacap.org/AACAP/Policy_Statements/2022/AACAP_Policy_Statement_Increased_Suicide_Among_Black_Youth_US.aspx. [Accessed 14 May 2024].

6. For more on this topic, see Kyra Aurelia Alessandrini's report in *Time* magazine: Alessandrini, K. A. (2021), 'Suicide Among Black Girls Is a Mental Health Crisis Hiding in Plain Sight', *Time:* https://time.com/6046773/black-teenage-girls-suicide/ [Accessed 19 October 2023].

7. Shapiro, T. M. (2004), *The Hidden Cost of Being African American: How Wealth Perpetuates Inequality.* New York: Oxford University Press.

Awesomeness

1. Sturm V. E., et al. (2022), 'Big smile, small self: Awe walks promote prosocial positive emotions in older adults', *Emotion*, 22(5): 1044-1058.

Drawing On Your Strengths

1. Cheng, X., et al. (2020), 'Measuring character strengths as possible protective factors against suicidal ideation in older Chinese adults: a cross-sectional study', *BMC Public Health*, 20(1): 439.

2. Wyman, P. A., et al. (2010), 'An outcome evaluation of the Sources of Strength suicide prevention program delivered by adolescent peer leaders in high schools', *American Journal of Public Health*, 100(9): 1653–61.

3. https://www.viacharacter.org/science-of-character. [Accessed 14 May 2024].

4. Linley, A. (2008), *Average to A+: Realising Strengths in Yourself and Others*. Coventry: CAPP Press.

5. Linley, A., Willars, J., and Biswas-Diener, R., (2010), *The Strengths Book: Be Confident, Be Successful, and Enjoy Better Relationships by Realising the Best of You*. Coventry: CAPP Press.

6. Bannink, F. (2012). *Practicing Positive CBT: From Reducing Distress to Building Success*. Hoboken: Wiley-Blackwell.

The Bliss of Lists

1. Sawhney, V. (2022), 'Why We Continue to Rely on (and Love) To-Do Lists', *Harvard Business Review*: https://hbr.org/2022/01/why-we-continue-to-rely-on-and-love-to-do-lists> [Accessed 14 May 2024].

One Thing

1. Soga, M., et al. (2016), 'Gardening is beneficial for health: A meta-analysis', *Preventive Medicine Reports*, 5: 92–99; The American Institute of Stress (2022), 'Gardening may reduce stress, anxiety, depression': https://www.stress.org/news/gardening-may-reduce-stress-anxiety-depression/ [Accessed 12 June 2024]; Egerer, M., et al. (2022), 'Gardening can relieve human stress and boost nature connection during the COVID-19 pandemic', *Urban Forestry & Urban Greening*, 68: 127483.

Healing Through Devotion

1. Chatterjee, R. *The Four Pillar Plan: How to Relax, Eat, Move and Sleep Your Way to a Longer, Healthier Life*. London: Penguin Life.

We Are Each Other's Medicine

1. Tunçgenç, B., et al. (2023), 'Social bonds are related to health behaviors and positive well-being globally', *Science Advances*, 9(2): eadd3715; Herrando, C. and Constantinides, E. (2021), 'Emotional Contagion:

A Brief Overview and Future Directions', *Frontiers in Psychology*, 12: 712606.

2. Murthy, V. H. (2020), *Together: The Healing Power of Human Connection in a Sometimes Lonely World*. New York: HarperCollins.

3. Harandi, T. F., et al. (2017), 'The correlation of social support with mental health: A meta-analysis', *Electronic Physician*, 9(9): 5212–22; Tunçgenç, B., et al. (2023), 'Social bonds are related to health behaviors and positive well-being globally', *Science Advances*, 9(2): eadd3715; Office of the Surgeon General (2023), 'Our Epidemic of Loneliness and Isolation: The U.S. Surgeon General's Advisory on the Healing Effects of Social Connection and Community', Washington, D.C.: US Department of Health and Human Services: https://www.hhs.gov/ sites/default/files/surgeon-general-social-connection-advisory.pdf. [Accessed 14 May 2024].

4. Macrynikola, N., et al. (2018), 'Social connectedness, stressful life events, and self-injurious thoughts and behaviors among young adults', *Comprehensive Psychiatry*, 80: 140–49.

5. Cohen, S. and McKay, G. (2020), 'Social Support, Stress, and the Buffering Hypothesis: A Theoretical Analysis.' In *Handbook of Psychology and Health, Volume IV*. Routledge. Chicago, pp. 253–267.

6. Hall, J. A., et al. (2023), 'Quality Conversation Can Increase Daily Well-Being', *Communication Research*: https://doi. org/10.1177/00936502221139363.

Other People Matter

1. Kramer, A. D. I., et al. (2014), 'Experimental evidence of massive-scale emotional contagion through social networks', *Proceedings of the National Academy of Sciences of the United States of America*, 111(24): 8788–90.

Bearing Witness

1. Johnson, J. (2010), 'The Power of Bearing Witness', HuffPost: https:// www.huffpost.com/entry/the-power-of-bearing-witn_b_721210 [Accessed 9 November 2023].

Intentional Friendship

1. Fisher, L. B., et al. (2015), 'From the Outside Looking In: Sense of Belonging, Depression, and Suicide Risk', *Psychiatry*, 78(1): 29–41.

Positive Communities

1. Baumeister, R. F., and Leary, M. R. (1995), 'The need to belong: Desire for interpersonal attachments as a fundamental human motivation', *Psychological Bulletin*, 117(3): 497–529.

2. McQuaid, M., et al. (2018), 'A character strengths-based approach to positive psychology coaching'. In: Green, S. and Palmer, S. (eds.), *Positive Psychology Coaching in Practice*. Abingdon: Routledge, pp.71–79.

Young People

1. Lopez, S. J. (2014), *Making Hope Happen: Create the Future You Want for Yourself and Others*. New York: Atria Books.

2. Cutler, D. M., et al. (2001), 'Explaining the Rise in Youth Suicide'. In: Gruber, J. (ed.), *Risky Behavior among Youths: An Economic Analysis*. Chicago: University of Chicago Press, pp.219–70.

3. Ebreo, J. E. S. (2023), 'A Study on Locus of Hope and Suicide Ideation among Undergraduate Students in the Philippines', *International Journal For Multidisciplinary Research*, 5(4).

The Optimist Creed

1. Larson, C. (1912), *Your Forces and How to Use Them*. New Literature Publishing Company.

Photo by: Bry Penney

About the Author

Niyc Pidgeon is an award-winning Positive Psychologist, international keynote speaker, certified coach, leading business mentor, and award-winning author. She is the founder of global online education brand Unstoppable Success® and the creator of the Positive Psychology Coach Academy Certification®.

After losing three close friends to suicide, Niyc felt called to share the potentially life-saving tools of Positive Psychology with as many people as possible. She is on a mission to make the world more mentally healthy, and she envisions a future where suicide no longer exists.

🌐 **niyc.com**

f **@niycpidgeon**

📷 **@niycpidge**